## Even People Who Disagree on Everything Agree on Adam Carolla!

"As the revolution reaches its final, most humorless stage, there's no better, braver, or more insightful observer than Adam Carolla. You may feel despondent about what's happening right now. This book will remind you that you should also be amused."

—TUCKER CARLSON

"Adam and I agree on absolutely *nothing*, but he's a sharp, smart, funny guy to disagree with. And there's a human heart under all the gruffness, snark, and melted cheese."

—PATTON OSWALT

"Adam Carolla has been leading the fight against politically correct 'woke' culture since before it was cool. His latest book is a must read for all common-sense Americans who are sick and tired of living in a bubble-wrapped world filled with safe spaces and trigger warnings."

—DONALD TRUMP JR.

"Adam has done it again! In this book he's managed to make me laugh at one moment, then cry out 'What an idiot!' in the next. His own blue-collar mastery of the language invites the reader into the conversation—just like the podcast—so much so that I breezed through the book in only one sitting on the toilet."

—BRYAN CRANSTON

"Within these pages, you will find written proof that Adam Carolla is insane. Buy this for your uncle."

—JIMMY KIMMEL

"Adam has written a funny, insightful book with a powerful message a bunch of people will manage to be offended by without reading it."

—TIM ALLEN

"Adam Carolla is the sort of blue-collar, sit-at-the-end-of-the-bar, sort-of intellectual I enjoy. With an impressive lexicon of metaphors and cultural references he paints hilarious pictures that will keep you entertained for hours. I really enjoyed this book."

—JAY LENO

"In my view, Adam Carolla is the wittiest observer of contemporary American life in our generation. This book is yet another example of his uniqueness. I can only advise you not to read *I'm Your Emotional Support Animal* in public, as you will laugh out loud so often, people will begin staring at you."

—DENNIS PRAGER

"Adam Carolla is a liar, a whore, a swindler, a degenerate, and borderline illiterate. But he knows a lot about cars. I mean, a lot."

—ALEC BALDWIN

"The Aceman has done it again. Nobody helps us all stay sane while giving us a much needed laugh quite like Adam Carolla. And I'm not just saying that because he asked me to."

—RICH EISEN

## Also by Adam Carolla

*I'M YOUR*
# Emotional
## SUPPORT ANIMAL

# I'm Your Emotional
# SUPPORT ANIMAL

NAVIGATING OUR
**ALL WOKE, NO JOKE**
CULTURE

## ADAM CAROLLA

Post Hill
PRESS

A POST HILL PRESS BOOK

I'm Your Emotional Support Animal:
Navigating Our All Woke, No Joke Culture
© 2020 by Adam Carolla
All Rights Reserved

ISBN: 978-1-64293-588-2
ISBN (eBook): 978-1-64293-589-9

Cover photography by Mohr Mohr
Creative direction & design by Danny Klein,
    DKLEINDESIGN + CREATIVE, LLC
Interior design & composition, Greg Johnson, Textbook Perfect

This is a work of nonfiction. All people, locations, events, and situations
are portrayed to the best of the author's memory.

**Post Hill Press**
New York • Nashville
posthillpress.com

Published in the United States of America

# Contents

# Preface

## No Apologies

This preface is going to be about not having prefaces. It drives me nuts that in our new all "woke" culture, everyone is scared shitless of the left and feels the need to preface any comment that could potentially offend with, "I work with many Hispanics. I have Latino heritage if you go back three generations," before they go on to talk about the chaos at the border, or "I have daughters. I'm a married man," before they speak on gender-related issues. It shows just how fucking petrified of the Twitter mob every public figure is nowadays. The fact that leftists have talked good people who've never harmed anyone into giving preemptive apologies to nutjobs is outrageous.

Consequently, I'm starting with a warning. I'm not going to apologize for anything in this book. I'm not going to qualify anything in this book. If you don't like something in this book, you can kiss my hairy ass. I'm like a country that lets the world know it doesn't negotiate with terrorists who take hostages. Guess what happens? Less hostages get taken. So I'm making a mark now. No fucking apologies. As the great Dr. Jordan Peterson said on my podcast, "You can't apologize to a mob."

This is all about the progressive movement. Think about those two words. "Progressive." "Movement." They mean it's never going to stop. It starts by moving toward real problems, but when the people in the movement run out of real problems, they still need to keep progressing, keep moving, and that's where we're at now. Dig this comparison: smoking. People used to be able to go into restaurants and smoke. They would light up at the table with impunity. They'd order up a steak with a side of Winstons. They'd be blowing smoke onto their entrée and into their kids' faces, and no one would say shit. Then some ancestor to today's progressive woke assholes said, "Hey, you can't smoke in the restaurant. Let's make a smoking section for you." The smokers got their cigarettes, their ashtrays, their steaks, and their martinis and went off to the smoking section. Then the woke douchebag showed up in the smoking section and said, "Hey, we can't have you smoking in the restaurant. I know there's a smoking section, but the smoke is wafting over into the main dining room. Why don't you just smoke at the bar?" All the smokers went, "Okay," and moved to the bar. Then the PC pussy said, "Hey, I know we said you could smoke at the bar, but now you have to go outside." The smokers put on their jackets and went outside to the patio. Then the progressive prick said, "You've got to get off the property and go out to the sidewalk." And they moved to the sidewalk. Then Captain Cocksucker said, "You're too close to the door. You're not outside enough. Go to the park." Except now there's no smoking in the park. So everyone went, "Fuck it, I'm vaping." And then the self-appointed societal hall monitor said, "Okay, that's illegal now, too." The question is: Do they hate cigarette smoke, or do they love telling people what to do? I think you know the answer to that one. I'm not a gun guy, but I'll tell you who figured this shit out: the NRA. The woke douche from the progressive movement said, "Hey, man, do you really need a grenade launcher on your M16?" and the NRA guy said, "How the fuck else am I gonna light my cigarette?"

They laid down a hard line. Charlton Heston declared you'd only get his gun from his cold, dead hands. (I hope Chuck was buried with a rifle just to test this theory. By the way, "from my cold, dead hands" is also my stance on masturbation.) The point is, smokers gave an inch and eventually lost a Marlboro mile.

It's the same with feeding the apology monster on social media. If you don't give people immediate gratification, they move on. These are the kids who got everything they wanted. They're a bunch of grown-up Veruca Salts demanding an Oompa Loompa *now*! If you just wait them out, they'll move on to their next target. What they want is for *you* to make *them* feel like *heroes* for forcing *you* to apologize. It's a power trip. If they try to wring you like a bar rag to get tears out of you and you come up dry, they move on. Never apologize. I'm not a resident of MAGA country, but I gotta give the devil his due. This is one thing Trump has gotten right, unlike firing me from *The Celebrity Apprentice*. (More on that and the Trump effect on our culture in chapter two.) Notice that no one ever asks Trump for an apology. They call him Hitler or call for impeachment, but they never call for an apology because they know they'll never get it.

When Dr. Drew's kids were young, he brought them by my place to get a little carpentry help from "the Ace Man" on their pinewood derby cars. I busted out the oscillating spindle sander and got to work. After a couple of hours, it was time to leave. At the end of the driveway, Drew said to the boys, "Now thank Mr. Carolla for his time." One of the eight-year-olds said, "We already thanked him in the garage." Drew said, "Well, thank him again." The kid argued back, and eventually it escalated to Drew's using the stern dad voice. "Thank him. *Now!*" I said, "Hey, Drew, you know what's ruining the moment? You shouting at your kids demanding they thank me." The spirit of the moment was gone. It's the same with forced apologies. The force defeats the purpose. You can't demand that someone do something they should do spontaneously.

We've all seen the athletes, politicians, and celebrities who get caught doing something stupid, like cheating on their wives. First off, why do *I* need the apology? Apologize to your old lady and move on. Frankly, I was kinda rooting for you and your cock. I'd be disappointed if the Lamar Odoms of the world weren't out banging around. Whenever this happens, the first reaction is always the real reaction. They seem confused and defensive. Then some publicist or manager gets ahold of them and scripts a lame non-apology for them to deliver at a press conference in a tone that seems like they just got a dose of methadone. Because that's what publicists get paid to do. No publicist has the balls to instruct their client to drop their pants and tell everyone to suck their dick. Instead, they craft a mea culpa for their client full of platitudes about how they've grown from this teachable moment and how they are going to take some time to reflect and be with their family. Bullshit. They're going to take some time not with their family but away from the media until it moves on to the next outrage du jour.

Someone could make a couple bucks starting a business, like those guys who write term papers for lazy, shitty students. Hire a couple of studious Asian kids to crank out stock apologies for when a celebrity's mistress comes out of the woodwork, or when they get caught at a "massage parlor," or that long-lost tape of them using the N-word surfaces. (Personally, I'd order the combo platter that covers all three of those.) A good publicist would recognize that the news cycle has about the same longevity as a fruit fly, and if they just keep their client out of the spotlight for seventy-two hours it'll all go away. That apology is like putting out a saucer of milk on your back steps for a feral cat. It's just going to keep it coming back for more "meow-trage."

I have a rich history of not apologizing, and I'm not going to start now. Many years ago I said something that offended my mother. Honestly, I can't remember what it was, but I do recall saying that it was a misunderstanding or that she had misinterpreted it. She replied that I should just apologize and we could move on. I said that I wouldn't. She asked why not. I told her if I apologized it would give credibility to this offense that I never intended. An apology is an admission of guilt. It implies I had malice in my heart. If she misunderstood me, that's on her. She continued to browbeat me for an apology. I wanted to ask, "Is your end goal to get me to shout, 'I'm sorry, your cuntness. I apologize. There. Can you die now!?' Because that's where this is headed." But I held back and held out. I wasn't going to legitimize her fake grievance. If I'm not going to apologize to my own mother for offenses in her head, I'm certainly not going to apologize to some asshole nineteen-year-old gender studies major on Twitter.

I don't understand the psychology of this. Let's say someone calls you fat. You demand an apology, and they give it to you. You're still fat. Nothing has changed. If you feel better about yourself after a forced apology, you must be really into dry humping and tofu, because both are just as satisfying.

You know what? I will end with one apology. I'm sorry for giving our shitty society too much benefit of the doubt. I wrote a book a decade ago called *In Fifty Years We'll All Be Chicks*, and

I was wrong. I was off by about forty-one years. I should never have allowed us that much hope. George Orwell gets all the praise for writing *1984*, but he wrote that in 1949. My pessimistic predictions came true much faster. Who's the genius now, George? People should constantly be bothering me and Mike Judge, who predicted humanity's current downfall in the brilliant opening ten minutes of *Idiocracy*, and picking our brains about what the future holds. My baseline, my factory default setting, is right. I can be very right and super right, but I'm never wrong. So grab a seat, preferably a toilet seat, as reading about how our society is going down the shitter will be good reading for when you're on the shitter. Over the next eight chapters, I'll show just how far we have fallen in such a short period of time, and I'll make some new predictions for our not-so-bright future. Get it on!

# Chapter 1

## Support Dogs
## and the Death of Dignity

Anyone who listens to my podcast or has read my books knows I don't support the animals who have support animals. I traveled the entire country with Dr. Drew in the '90s and never saw a single dog on a plane. It was not allowed and, therefore, people didn't do it. Our biology hasn't changed that much since I was on MTV. People didn't start suffering from a new illness stemming from dramatically low levels of dog dander in their system. We just got softer. But since the time I wrote about this in *President Me*, people taking their dogs on flights, much like the planes they're on, took off. I wrote then about two service dogs fighting at my feet in first class. Since then, I'm sure we've had more aerial dogfights than Pappy Boyington. ( Google It ) **bit.ly/ESA-Pappy**

It used to be just white chicks with lapdogs, but no more. For the record, and to let me garner some goodwill with the brothers before I bash them in upcoming chapters, this is the domain of whitey. I have never seen a black or brown person with an emotional support dog. Maybe someday there will be a Jackie, or Jackée, Robinson who will break the color barrier on emotional support dogs, but for now this is a first-world honkey problem.

This virus has now spread from batty white broads to dudes. I was dejected in 2015 when I did my daily due diligence of watching *TMZ*—because I'm an intellectual heavyweight—and saw Henry Cavill, star of the recent *Superman* movies, leaving LAX with his emotional support mutt. It's a bird, it's a plane…with Superman getting off it with his fucking dog?! Superman. You couldn't find someone in better shape than the guy who plays Superman. I'd understand if it was an old former ingénue like Jane Fonda with a Maltese in her purse, but this is an able-bodied thirty-two-year-old male action star. No one requires a service dog less than this guy. He's a rich actor. This is Superman. He doesn't even need a dog accessory to get blown.

Then in 2016 at O'Hare airport in Chicago, I saw a woman with a schnauzer named Rhino. I know its name because I asked. (Note: If I ever come up to you in an airport and act interested, prepare to be podcast fodder.) She told me she had named him Rhino "because he charges everyone." Sure, just what you're looking for in the aisle of a 737. She then proceeded to tell me he was an emotional support animal. At some point people crossed over from "service" dogs to "support" dogs. It even had a little vest that read "ESA." Eventually the vests will just read "FU." She then proceeded to say she had gone through a rough patch emotionally and Rhino made it better. I'm not taking that away from her. I had a cat named Norman that was far and away the best part of my childhood. Anyone who knows my podcast has heard all the tales of the pups I've had—Lotzi, Molly, and now Phil E. Cheesesteak. But I leave Phil at home when I fly. He's barely housebroken. He's definitely not plane-broken. (Phil, by the way, is the dog lying across my lap on the cover of this book.)

Later that year at the St. Louis airport, I saw a very able-bodied woman traveling with not one but two service dogs. Do you have double the anxiety? One's not enough? No special vest on either of them, by the way. She didn't even bother attempting to make it look like she had trained these dogs or that they provided any service other than to this bitch's ego. Eventually Cruella de Vil is going to get on a Delta flight with 101 fucking Dalmatians.

I've only seen it escalate since then. Mark my words, after the next major plane crash we have, they are going to count the dogs in the news story like they separate the passengers and crew. It'll be reported as 145 passengers, 6 crew members, and 11 dogs, and all the dumb chicks will be more upset about the dogs.

(BTW) An offshoot of this, and definitely the domain of the middle-aged, middle-class, white chick is FCHD. You'll find out what that stands for in a few sentences. Last year I was walking Phil around the neighborhood. It was not blistering hot, but it was warm. I made a quick stop at the supermarket to get an iced tea and did what a normal human being does: left Phil tied up outside with his leash around a pole because, like planes, dogs have no fucking business in a supermarket. I came out twelve minutes later, and some Good Samaritan had given Phil a bowl of water. (That person probably stepped over six homeless people on the way to do it, because human beings have fucked-up wiring about how they treat people versus how they treat animals, especially in L.A., where we treat animals like people and the government treats people like animals.)

I knew it was a chick because this was the third time it had happened. If I walk Phil around my neighborhood at noon on a Tuesday, three broads will offer him water. On two separate occasions, women pulled over to offer Phil a bottle of water. To be clear, they weren't walking their dogs when they came up to us. They pulled their SUVs over and rolled down the window to offer Phil a frosty-cold bottle of $H_2O$.

I believe this is a classifiable disorder that should be published in medical and psychological journals—Feminine Canine Hydration Disorder. FCHD, pronounced "fucked," is a type of dementia in which the brain of the female deteriorates beginning at age thirty-eight and the only remaining fully functional portion is the part concerned with a dog's water intake.

I can speak about this affliction because it has literally been a pox on my house. When it comes to ranking her effectiveness at many things in life—such as cleaning, taking care of me, or cooking—my wife, Lynette, would not get five stars. But when it comes to being on top of Phil's water bowl, you would need to add a sixth star. My wife suffers from FCHD, and I'm a survivor. 😁

## A Tale of Terriers, Terrazzo, and Turds

We're enabling this shit, and now that shit is on the ground. Lately I'm seeing "Service Animal Relief Area" signs in airports all around the country. No smoking and no shampoo over 3.5 ounces, but there's a place for your pooch to drop a deuce.

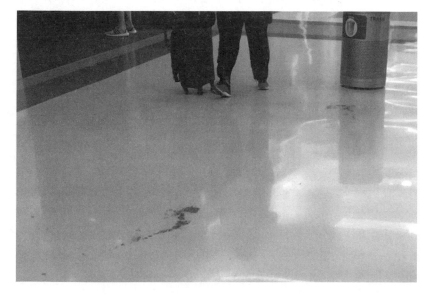

That's if they even make it to the "relief area." In 2018 I was traveling to Cleveland to do a little stand-up, and on my way to the gate at the airport, I came across a squatty Guatemalan woman on her hands and knees scrubbing the floor. She had the cones out, gloves on, and the mop and bucket nearby. At first I didn't think anything of it, but as I kept walking toward my gate I saw more mess.

I was looking at a half acre of shit-streaked terrazzo. Some dog had the runs and sprayed it every twenty feet through the whole goddamn terminal. This covered well over 150 feet. I wouldn't even have been able to get a tape measure out to determine the damage. I'd have to bust out one of those wheels that California Highway Patrol uses to measure skid marks at an accident.

Good thing I have a hypervigilance disorder, because I saw multiple people with their earbuds in and looking at their phones and not even noticing that they had just wheeled their Samsonites through doggy diarrhea. I doubled back and talked to the Guatemalan airport worker and asked her if it was dog shit, as I suspected. She laughed and said it was, which pissed me off because I want everyone to be as outraged about this as I am. Especially the person who's cleaning up the mess from some asshole's dog's asshole.

It should be clear by now, I don't think you should have your dog at the airport at all, never mind if it has the runs, but let's move past that. I'll even be kind and give you a pass on the first salvo from your dog's tuchus. I know from Phil that dogs eat things they shouldn't eat and shit where they shouldn't shit. But on the second shot of shit squirt, that becomes *your* responsibility. You should have to clean your pooch's poop. But we've established that you're a narcissist by virtue of the fact that you brought your dog to the airport in the first place, so of course you're not going to think it's your job to clean up your little princess's turd explosion. That's for some serf to do.

Just imagine if this happened on the plane. They'd be forced to turn it around and have an emergency landing, ruining the day of all the sane people just trying to get to Phoenix. If we had a chart that showed the number of emotional support dogs on planes, it would go from nothing fifteen years ago, climb slowly to a few ten years ago, and then spike in the past five years. If we had a chart that also tracked fistfights with flight attendants, attempts to open emergency doors midflight while high on prescriptions, defecations on drink carts, and generally doing shit that diverts flights, it would be the same fucking graph. It would be an exact correlation, because the root cause is the same—more emotionally unstable dickheads on planes. We need to fix this problem. If your psyche is so compromised that you can't fly without your dog, you should be forced to take a bus. It's called Greyhound for a reason. Get your hound and get on the fucking bus.

## Menagerie Airlines

Since 2015, it's gone insane. We've moved from carrying on simple domesticated housepets to exotic creatures. Planes are becoming arks. Fucking Noah is walking down the aisle with two of every creature on earth.

You would have thought that around the time the donkey was replaced by the pickup truck that we would no longer be using service animals. It'd be interesting to get a time machine and talk to a farmer from 1870 and say, "One hundred and fifty years from now, we'll still be using service animals, but not for plowing fields and turning a grindstone."

"Oh, so it will just be oxen pulling a wagon across the Great Plains?"

"Well, it will be for travel but not quite. You know those hysterical women you give laudanum and lock in the sanitarium? In the future we give them turkeys, pigs, and miniature horses to make them feel better and let them roam about the country in magical flying machines."

His head would explode.

Every flight has become a barnyard in the sky. Here is just a partial list of animals that have been on planes and, thus, in the news.

Snake: I've actually seen more than one of these on the news. I sleep like a baby knowing that anyone who has an emotional support snake will eventually have that snake strangle them in their sleep. That thing you hand-feed mice to will eventually turn on you in the middle of the night for no reason.

Turkeys and ducks: In *President Me*, and later in my movie *Road Hard*, I did a bit about my service pelican, Gilligan, who would walk the aisle scooping up and gulping down all the service chihuahuas. Little did I know that a mere two years later, my farcical comedy bit would come to life with people bringing their fowl onto flights, though you could have a nice "Who's on First?"–style bit if the flight was heading to Turkey.

Pig: Then there was the news story about the US Airways flight that thankfully removed a pig. They made her take her emotional support hog off as well. (See what I did there?) This crackpot had a seventy-pound porker on a leash but had to get off the flight when it shit in the aisle before they could even take off. Unless the plane ends up crashing in the Andes with you and your soccer team, and the pig delays by a couple days the descent into cannibalism, it has no fucking business on a plane.

Miniature pony: Permit me to get on my high horse and talk a little shit about your low horse. The notion of breeding a miniature horse flies in the face of horse breeding in general. These are supposed to be tall, majestic creatures. They're meant to be barrel-raced or pulling the Budweiser wagon through a small town, not pulling a lesbian who's filed her seventh slip-and-fall lawsuit this year through an airport. It doesn't make sense. No one is trying to breed Brad Williams and Dikembe Mutombo. ( 🔍 Google It ) **bit.ly/ESA-Brad**

Where are you going that you can bring a horse with you? You're eventually going to get off the plane, right? Are you going to hail an Uber and stuff the pigmy pony in the trunk? Which Holiday Inn are you going to that allows Tiny Trigger to sleep in your room? There's no lawn jockey for you to hitch up your fun-size foal to while you take in a Broadway show. Horses are meant to be traveled upon, not with. I have a novel idea. How about you get on your horse and ride to your destination so I can enjoy my flight and not feel like I'm at a 4H event?

Wallaby: A teen from Portland had a wallaby named Momo to deal with panic attacks. I know, shocking. Usually the people of Portland are known for their stout, blue-collar grittiness. She would carry it in a Babybjörn-style pouch. When I was a kid, my parents wouldn't let me have a dog. This girl's got a fucking marsupial. The only upside to this one is that when someone slips in its shit at the airport, you could offer them ten thousand dollars to name the animal it came from. Given a hundred guesses, they'd never get it. Only in this pathetic era could we potentially have that game show. I'd call it *Name That Dook*.

Because these people are nuts, they can have anything for an emotional support animal. We are not that far from, "This is my emotional support abalone. I don't fly anywhere without Shelly."

Here's my point. This is more than a pet peeve, pun intended. It's not just about the dogs. The dogs are just the canary in the coal mine, if I can mix my animal metaphors. They are an eerie harbinger of worse to come. As you'll see in the rest of this book, I don't have a lot of optimism for our culture, and this support animal stuff is a leading indicator. The increase in support dogs on planes is directly proportional to the decrease of dignity in our society.

People are sad, pathetic, and weak. I've never understood why people advertise that they are so soft. I would rather cut off my dick and my pinkie and sew my pinkie where my dick goes and my dick where my pinkie goes than admit I'm so emotionally weak that I need a pet in order to board a plane. What I've come to realize is that in today's society, being a victim, overcoming racism, and being "brave" and "fearless" are currency. In the '70s, it was "Let your freak flag fly." In the 2020s, it's "Let your weak flag fly." It's a competition to see who is more "oppressed" and who faces more "adversity." And it's a competition where everyone is a loser, especially our society.

This is all mental weakness and lack of character. I guarantee that if you offered most of these batty broads vouchers for free flights to San Jose in exchange for leaving their pooches behind, they'd take them in a second. So how fucking necessary can they be? Some of these losers would do it for an extra bag of cashews. That wouldn't work with pancreatic cancer. A voucher for a first-class flight to Denver isn't going to make that go away. But the softness they have in their heads that causes them to need dogs in their laps to be able to fly can go away as quickly as the farts coming out of said dogs' asses evaporate into the coach cabin.

Speaking of cabin air, what about smokers on planes? Why aren't we catering to them like we cater to people with dog addictions? We all know there's no tampering with, disabling, or destroying the smoke detectors on flights, but what about guys like the velvet-throated Mike Dawson, the announcer on my podcast, who needs a hit of nicotine every few minutes. He's shit out of luck, because we've decided vaping is bad and dogs are good. You could easily argue that, medically, Dawson needs that nicotine in his lungs more than some dingbat needs Benji on her lap. He's forced to wear NicoDerm while some chick is flying with a pachyderm. He'd never be allowed to have an emotional support Camel.

In 2018, I was flying on Southwest Airlines, from Burbank to Sacramento. At Burbank Airport, you walk out onto the tarmac rather than on a jetway. It's a classy place. I saw a guy with a medium-size dog on a leash, no handle, no special vest. He briskly walked across the tarmac and got on the flight. There wasn't a single thing wrong with this guy. The kicker was that a woman in a wheelchair trailed behind him. This doggy-daddy douchebag didn't even have the dignity to fake a limp. He just strolled right past a woman with a clear disability. Actually, I stand corrected; this guy did have a disorder. A personality disorder.

It's not just the pet owners who have lost their dignity. It used to be that you'd have to get a note from your doctor, even if that doctor was a quack or just didn't feel like dealing with your crazy ass so he wrote a note just to shut you up. Now there are online "doctors" who will write that note without ever meeting you or your mutt. It's brazen. I've seen ads for "ESA letters for both housing and travel...just $98." Is that what your dignity is worth, Doctor Nick Riviera? I would rather hang out with a doctor who specializes in penis enlargement and only uses cells from cadavers of veterans who died in combat than one of these licensed psychologists who's sold his soul to supply letters to fruitcakes so they can bring their pets on planes. People who give blowjobs for crack have more dignity than these assholes. At least the crack whores didn't pay for medical school.

We are so eager to part with our dignity for a couple of bucks and some convenience. I'm not saying this just for me or for society. I'm saying it for all of you weak-minded people.

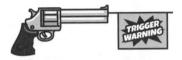

You are declaring from on high, literally thirty thousand feet high, that you are so precariously wired and emotionally fragile that you need a dog with you at all times to make you feel better. You've externalized the problem. You've given a creature that eats its own shit the power over whether or not you can handle life. That's not good for you in the long run. That is not going to teach you resilience or how to overcome your fears. It's only going to reinforce them and continue to make you feel like a victim. You don't need a therapist to write you a note so you can bring a petting zoo on the plane; you need that therapist to do their fucking job and help you get better. All anyone has is their dignity. The one thing you have your whole life, the one thing that doesn't have to change as you get older and fatter, is dignity. That is your constant. If you give that up, you're fucked. Your dog may be carry-on, but you have checked your dignity.

# Chapter 2

# The Obligatory Trump Chapter

Let's get this out of the way. It's obvious that the current hyper-escalation of the "woke" culture is a direct reaction to the Trump presidency. It would be impossible to write a book about our social and cultural decline without addressing President Trump, even though a lot of readers are going to be mad that I'm giving the devil his due. I'm not saying I'm a huge Donald Trump fan. No MAGA hat has ever covered my Brillo hair and, as you'll soon read, I've had personal experiences with Trump, both positive and negative, that inform my opinions about him. I knew him long before he was president. I thought he was a blowhard then, and being in the White House hasn't changed that, but I'm not going to ignore things he has done that I agree with just because he did them, as many of my friends in California do.

Let me also make a caveat that at the time the first draft of this book was being written, the impeachment inquiry over Trump's call with Ukraine's president looking for dirt on Joe Biden and his son Hunter was going on. As this sentence is being written Trump is getting acquitted by the Senate. The book still needs to be printed. By the time it gets into your hot little hands who knows what will be going on? Nancy Pelosi and Adam Schiff could find, or create, something else to impeach him for, he could have Rudy Giuliani going through their trash looking for embarrassing shit to tweet about, or he could nuke Denmark just for the fuck of it. One thing we know is that Trump creates scandals like I move my bowels. It's pretty much once a day, twice if there's a second cup of coffee. I'm not going to start breaking down all the sex scandals, cabinet secretary firings, and typo-filled two a.m. tweets. There are plenty of other books on the market for that. I would just like to make one suggestion for a scandal I'd like to see before the end of 2020. This coming Thanksgiving, when it comes time to do the traditional pardoning of the turkey, I think Trump should pull out a gold-plated .45 and put a slug right into the thing. That would be totally on brand, and his fans would lap it up.

## Adam Carolla: President Predictor

It's been noted that I actually predicted this administration in my book *President Me*. I wrote this in 2014:

> *Everyone laughed when Donald Trump thought about throwing his comb-over into the ring in the last election. But we live in a country where 45 percent of people believe in guardian angels and think Elvis is still alive. Why wouldn't we elect Trump? He'd certainly make the White House a lot classier—a big picture of himself in the Oval Office where George Washington's portrait used to hang and a lot of gold-leaf toilet seats.*

What I don't get enough credit for is that I actually called it eight years before the election on my morning radio show. In March 2008, my newsgirl Teresa Strasser played a clip of "The Donald" telling people that in order to make money, they have to love what they do. After making fun of that idiotic cliché, I said the following.

*He's going to be president in eight years. You understand that, everybody? You understand Donald Trump is going to be president. He'll be president one day. It'll be in our lifetime....*

I also predicted that Ivanka would be in the administration, though I said Trump would name her "Secretary of Class" and that Don Jr. would be "Chancellor in Charge of Losers" to make sure there are no losers. To be fair, I was wrong when I said he would no longer be with Melania because "she will have seen her thirty-eighth birthday by then." I've still got a fighting chance on two more predictions from that segment: that, due to his taste in décor, all streetlights would be replaced by chandeliers, and that he'd turn Cuba into a world-class exclusive golf resort.

I don't think even Donald Trump predicted Donald Trump was going to be president. I would love to get a time machine and stand outside the *Access Hollywood* bus where our future leader was engaged in some locker room talk with Billy Bush. As soon as they got off, I'd say, "I'm from the future, and I've got some good news and some bad news. What you guys were just talking about is going to be all over the media. And one of you is going to be president, and the other is going to get fired over this and be at home crying and watching daytime TV. Any guess who's who?"

( BTW ) Billy Bush was Me Too'd before Me Too was a thing. In fact, maybe that's where the phrase came from. The "grab 'em by the pussy" tape came out and people started talking about firing Trump from the Republican ticket, but Billy got fired instead and he said, "Me too?" Did he really have to get fired? I get why we're pissed at Trump, but I don't know why you needed to shit-can Billy as collateral damage. It's so disingenuous when we hold people to standards we couldn't achieve ourselves. He was trying to do a segment with a larger-than-life figure who was a major TV star at the time. He laughed at something that guest said. Was he supposed to storm off the bus like the old lady from a Marx Brothers movie and say, "Well, I never!" Plus, Billy Bush doesn't do anything. He shouldn't have been fired because he never should have been hired. That's like firing a teleprompter. He has no discernable talent other than being able to look handsome and read stuff about the Kardashians. Not to mention that this was being secretly recorded. Yes, he had a microphone on, but trust me, as someone who's had plenty of lavalier mics clipped on, you immediately forget they're there. And they're supposed to be turned off when you're prepping for your segment. I'm sure there's some tape of me out there saying horrible things about my wife and kids in addition to the hours and hours of my widely distributed podcasts in which I say horrible things about my wife and kids. 😬

Since I successfully prognosticated this presidency, let me put on my turban and gaze into the future at some other possible "celeb-ridents."

**Michael Strahan:** He just never stops climbing. He's charming, can read a teleprompter, works his ass off, and checks the racial box.

**Dwayne "The Rock" Johnson:** Another ex-jock with a crazy work ethic. Perfect for our crazy troubled times, he's a got a built-in campaign slogan: "Solid as The Rock." It'll be great in the debate when he arches his eyebrow and says, "Can you smell what The Rock is cooking? I'll tell you what The Rock is cooking. A three percent increase in the gross domestic product, a six percent middle-class tax cut and proportional increase to the childcare credit!!!!!!!!!!" That son of a bitch could pay off half the national debt with what he's pulling in for just *The Fast and the Furious* movies. Ooooh…running mate Jason Statham. I can see the bumper sticker: "Hobbs/Shaw 2024." Let's make this happen, people.

**Kim Kardashian:** She's clearly ambitious enough, but if she doesn't end up jamming her big booty behind the Resolute desk, I actually think she might end up on the Supreme Court. At least that's what I'm hoping for. She's trying to be a lawyer now, and she's already had some success with prison reform. If Trump can be president, why can't Kim Kardashian be a Supreme Court justice? It might be difficult for her to have a job where she's not being filmed, though. The reason I'm pulling for this is because there's already a sex tape of her out there. Imagine if you could instantly pull up bootleg porn of the chief justice of the Supreme Court on the internet. We'd be done as a nation. That would be peak America. I know there's a Ruth Bader Ginsburg movie on Netflix, but that shit's barely spankable.

**Clay Aiken:** He's already taken a stab at politics in his home state of North Carolina. Much like with *The Celebrity Apprentice* and *American Idol*, he didn't win but should have. He's an incredibly substantial person, as I learned in the few weeks I spent with him before I got booted off. You learn quickly from doing *The Celebrity Apprentice* who's got "it" and who doesn't. It's a little like the punt, pass, and kick competition. You can't be good at just one thing. They come in and throw you a task, and you have to decide who's the leader, which assignments fall on which people, all while keeping your cool. You have forty-eight hours to make a bunch of correct decisions under enormous pressure. Then you have to go into a boardroom and get reviewed. That's how all of life should operate, especially political leadership. You work hard and smart, and then are held accountable. The ability to delegate, work under stress, rise to challenges, and take criticism are all good presidential qualities, and, I'm telling you, Clay has them.

No matter who's next, I feel bad for them. Trump is going to be a tough act to follow—not because the shoes will be difficult to fill or that people won't be relieved to get back to some sense of normalcy, but because he will have tainted the office so much. If you sit in the Oval Office one or even two elections from now, you're still going to feel like I did when my first book debuted at #8 on the *New York Times* bestseller list. I looked up at #6 and saw it was *They Call Me Baba Booey*. Kinda ruined the moment.

## *The Celebrity Apprentice, The Marriage Ref,* and Personal Momentum

I worked with Donald Trump long before he came down his escalator and called Mexicans rapists. (He stole that bit from me, by the way.) Dig how surreal this time in our country is. One of the first times I met the man was in 2007, when I was interviewing him for my morning radio show. We were doing a *Celebrity Apprentice* premiere event at the Playboy Mansion. Yes, I interviewed the man who now occupies the most famous house in the country at the second-most-famous house in the country. Both are places, coincidentally, where Marilyn Monroe got plowed. The man whose hand I shook while naked chicks painted like Miller Lite bottles cavorted in the grotto is now in charge of our nukes. USA! USA! USA!

As far as my stint on *The Celebrity Apprentice* in 2012, I'll spare you the stories that don't involve The Donald. Let me just say this: I got jobbed—Steve Jobbed. I was told by the producers to do a Steve Jobs–style presentation, but when I did that, I got criticized for not using the rest of the team. You know all those Steve Jobs presentations where he brought out George Takei, Teresa Giudice, and Lou Ferrigno? Anyway, I got cut early but came back for the finale. The last two contestants were the aforementioned Clay Aiken and Arsenio Hall. (Just imagine, if we didn't live in such a racist and homophobic society, there'd be three gay guys and five black guys in the finale.) Arsenio picked me first for his team. For the final challenge, we had to produce a charity show, and I ended up having to roast Trump. He was standing eight feet away, so it wasn't like I could deliver it to the crowd. He's about six foot three, but his hair makes him nine feet tall. He sticks out. And he stands like his cock has elephantiasis, as if his ankles couldn't get closer than thirty-one inches. He stands like someone at high noon who's about to shout, "Draw!" So, not only am I delivering jokes about Trump to the thirteen million viewers watching at home, but I'm insulting the man to his face. Here's what I said: "People always ask me what Donald Trump is like. And I say, 'Picture Don King with crazier hair and a broken moral compass.' Seriously, that hair. Until you get up close and see it in person, you can't understand the majesty of it. It moves and breathes. It's got lungs. You ever see underwater footage of a kelp bed? It's like that. There are clownfish darting in and out." I think this is why Trump likes Kim Jong Un. He's the only other world leader with a shittier haircut. A lot of people call it a comb-over, but it doesn't just flop over like an omelet. It's more like soft-swirl ice cream.

Anyway, my Don King/Don Trump joke got a big laugh. From everyone but Trump. He was not pleased. Of all the things about himself that he labels "tremendous," sense of humor should not be one of them. The joke after that didn't land so well with the crowd: "Arsenio Hall. What a legend. The first African American to have a late-night talk show. He broke down so many barriers paving the way for Conan O'Brien, Jon Stewart, Jimmy Kimmel, Jimmy Fallon, Craig Kilborn, Craig Ferguson…" I stand by it.

> **BTW** You know two people who didn't watch that finale? My parents. They're not fans—of Trump or me. Since he has become president, they have denied and down-rounded my association with him every time it has come up. They took different roads but ended up at the same destination. A few years ago, shortly after he was elected, I was talking to my mom. She was hyperventilating about how Trump was going to get us into a war and

just start blowing stuff up. I told her not to worry about it, that I knew the guy and he wouldn't do that. She shot back, "Well, you don't really know him." I responded, "I've spent some time with him, I've interviewed him, I think a lot of it is an act." She kept at it. "You don't really *know* him." I found it odd that she was trying to talk her son out of the fact that he knew the president. Most parents would be proud. To be fair to my mom, she'd be equally dug in if I was talking about knowing Barack Obama. It's guilt by association. If I, her loser son, know them, then they can't be that good.

While my mom's angle was "You don't know him," my dad's was "That's great. Now let me do twenty minutes on why he's the worst human on the planet." He didn't even know who Trump was in 2016, and yet, at age eighty-something, he's completely triggered by him. He was apoplectic about "kids in cages." He was literally in fight-or-flight mode. He watches too much CNN. For the record, Dad, a cage would have been a major improvement in my life when I was a kid. In fact, I'm going to blow a call in to Trump right now to see if it's not too late to get separated from my family. 😁

I had another interaction with Trump before *The Celebrity Apprentice* that I think captures why he captured the White House. In March 2010 I was doing *The Marriage Ref*. For those of you who may not remember, that was a short-lived show hosted by the comedian Tom Papa, where celebrity guests mediated and judged marital disputes. The night I did it, the guests were me, Donald Trump, and Gloria Estefan. Again, think how crazy it is that the guy who was on par with me and the chick from Miami Sound Machine from a booking standpoint is now the most recognized person in the world. I bet nationally and internationally at this point, more people know his picture than Elvis or the Beatles.

Backstage before the show, I told him I watched *The Celebrity Apprentice*. He instantly launched into his sales pitch. He told me how great the numbers were and how the show was keeping NBC afloat. Then, during the taping, he leaned over and said, "Adam. This is going to be their highest-rated episode." Confidence. That's the point. I had no reason to believe it would even be moderately rated, but he said it as if he were willing it into existence. (For the record, it was not the highest-rated show of the season, as evidenced by the fact that I had to spend a few sentences earlier explaining what the show was.) This is what attracts people to Donald Trump. He has a way of speaking so confidently that you start to believe him. He's like a skilled prostitute. He makes you feel like the only person he's ever spoken to. For ten seconds, I felt better about myself and that, yes, it could be their highest-rated show. I felt like he was going to make my career great again. He also told me that earlier in the day he had been working on a big financial deal. I replied that earlier that day I had spent twenty minutes looking in my hotel minibar for something less than eight dollars. Then, backstage after the taping, he bragged about how Melania speaks five languages, and I thought, *Yeah, but none of them is English.*

Trump is either so narcissistic or such a good salesman that he thinks if he says it, it will be true. This guy lies about stuff that can easily be verified with a simple Google search. When presented with facts that prove him wrong, he calls them fake news. In our rapid-fire twenty-four-hour news cycle, people go with the first thing they hear, not the truth. Trump knows this. This is his appeal. He tells people what they want to hear. While trying to find the exact date for this story, I dug up Trump's tweet from that night. He said he was on "the panel of experts." I don't know that me and the Cuban chick who sang "Conga" in 1985 qualify as experts, but I'll take it.

> **Donald J. Trump** ✔
> @realDonaldTrump
>
> Tune in to The Marriage Ref onThursday night at 10 p.m. on NBC--I'm on the panel of experts along with Gloria Estefan & Adam Carolla.
>
> 3:12 PM · Apr 20, 2010

The guy knows how to strategically exaggerate. This is the same kind of personal momentum that you see in schlubby Jewish guys who are nailing hot blonde actresses. You look at them and think, *Why the fuck is she with him?* Then you talk to the guy and you see he's got charisma, confidence, and energy, and is not afraid to toot his own horn. Trump is the dumpy Jewish guy, and Ohio, Wisconsin, and Pennsylvania are the hot blondes. There's no reason they should be with him, but they are.

In 2016, I think people just wanted to shake things up. In comes master self-marketer Donald Trump to say, "I'm the guy." There've been five to eight movies made about Trump already, like *Bullworth* and *Dave,* where the plain-talking regular guy becomes president and shakes up the status quo, but they star Warren Beatty and Kevin Kline, not an orange sack of douche. Hollywood tries to get out ahead of things. Producers knew that the plain-talking, not-in-the-pocket-of-anybody politician was an appealing idea. They focus-tested it, and because it was Hollywood, they made him likable. Trump is the real, less attractive version of that. People were so desperate for someone who wasn't a canned-response, political robot that they elected a spray-tanned wrecking ball. Trump did with being uncouth what

Snoop Dogg did with weed. It's now expected. It's like Howard Stern. We anticipate and secretly want outrage. If Trump one day stopped tweeting "yo mama" snaps at world leaders and members of his own cabinet, we wouldn't know what to do. And he gets the whole "no apologies" thing I wrote about in the preface. Think about the Republican candidate who ran before him. Going from Mitt Romney to Trump is like going from a mug of Postum to a 23-ounce tall boy of Four Loko. Romney was a stiff. Obama was "no drama." Say what you will about Trump; he ain't boring. Admit it. You wouldn't want it any other way. Look at Mike Pence. Again, as this book goes to the printer, Trump has just dodged the impeachment bullet. Would any of you have really wanted a President Pence? Pence won't have dinner with a woman if it's not his wife. Trump won't have dinner with a woman unless it's not his wife. Pence doesn't drink, but neither does Trump, oddly enough. Why doesn't Trump drink? He has the face, hair, and golf clubs of someone who drinks. Golf was invented to give guys who don't want to be around their wives an opportunity to get day drunk. He looks and acts like an alcoholic. I'm going to work on this. We need to get him a red MAGA beer helmet.

Additionally, I think the election of Trump was a reaction to all the campus safe-space microaggression bullshit. Ironically, it has made it worse (more on that later), but back in 2016, there were lots of people in Michigan, Ohio, and Wisconsin who might have been in Hillary Clinton's basket of deplorables but instead voted against the basket of pussies our country was becoming. Blue-collar guys and gals' electing Trump was like a girl having revenge sex. They were saying, "We're not even attracted to this guy, but we're fucking him anyway just because he's not you."

There was also a schadenfreude aspect to his election. A certain percentage of his votes weren't pro-Trump; they were pro–*Saturday Night Live*. People wanted to see the parody. You have to remember, this is the same country that almost had Sanjaya winning the sixth season of *American Idol*. There are a lot of people who go to a fireworks show hoping the barge catches on fire.

And Trump reset the rules. There was a long period when submarine warfare was considered uncouth. It simply wasn't done. Until, like most innovations involving death, the Germans got involved. One sunken *Lusitania* later, everyone had to get in on it. Subs changed the playing field. So has Trump. It used to be unthinkable to throw shade at a political opponent on social media, talk about penis size at a debate, call other nations shitholes, involve rival candidates' kids, apply schoolyard nicknames or, literally, call bullshit at a rally. Trump didn't just change the game; he knocked over all the pieces and took a shit on the board.

This unpredictability is one of the things I like about Trump. Other tyrannical nations are now petrified of us. Just ask the smoking corpse of Qasem Suleimani if he saw that one coming. We have our own maniacal ruler with a finger, or perhaps his dick, on the button.

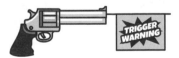

On that note, I offer a closing rant directed at the "Trump Derangement" people, especially those in Congress, running for president, and in the media. In case you, dear reader, don't know the term "Trump Derangement Syndrome," it applies to those who think Trump is an evil monster who can do no right—the people who, if Trump rescued a dozen puppies and children from a burning special-needs orphanage, would complain that he didn't wipe his feet on the way into the blazing building. I'm not blindly defending everything he's done, as others do. But I'm also not going to blindly turn every scandal into the *War of the Worlds* broadcast and join the chorus of boys and girls crying wolf. I don't think he's Superman, like the people at his rallies do, but I don't think he's Lex Luthor either. If you watch CNN or MSNBC, you'll see talking heads and Democratic politicians saying, "Our democracy is over. We're living in a dictatorship." Trump may be a dick, but he's not a dictator. Just because you don't like him doesn't make him Hitler.

As soon as the case for Russian collusion fell flat when the Mueller Report was released, liberals went through the five stages of grieving—denial, anger, bargaining, depression, and calling Trump a racist. They moved right on to the next line of attack. And then they got served up a new impeachment entrée, the quid pro quo with the Ukrainian president. As it unfolded I knew it would never bring Trump down. And I knew it didn't matter because the Democrats' strategy is more nefarious. The Trump Derangement crew doesn't actually have a plan. They're using all the scandals to cover their own ineptitude. They could put up a candidate with good policies or they could win another way: by keeping the noise meter pegged through all four years of his term. If they can keep that plate spinning until the next election, their candidate's platform can be, "I don't have any policies or plans, but don't you just want all this to stop?" They're trying to get us to a saturation point where we will vote for Pat Paulsen ( Google It ) **bit.ly/ESA-Pat** just to get it to end. They've got it to the point where we're praying for an earthquake in Ecuador or a ferry overturning in India just to have something different on the news. It's like when you end up yelling at your kid, "Fine! Have a goddamn Snickers bar for dinner. I don't fucking care. I just don't want to argue anymore." You give in to the constant nagging. That's what this is. This is the real quid pro quo. Quid: vote Trump out of office. Quo: we'll shut the fuck up.

To those of you thinking *I just want it to end*, me too. Not only the constant drumbeat of beat Trump, but also this chapter.

# Chapter 3

# It's Not All Good
in the Victimhood

The pearl-clutching-pussy thing went into high gear when Trump took office, but our toughness has slowly been eroding since even before I wrote *In Fifty Years We'll All Be Chicks*. There's plenty of blame to go around—the aforementioned support animals, politicians, the soon-to-be-mentioned news outlets, lawyers, race hustlers, and television, specifically the "true crime" shows and Lifetime movies designed to freak women out.

I noticed this starting to creep in soon after I had my kids. Hysterical hand-wringing from women has always existed, but it never really affected me. It came home to roost, however, when my kids came home from the hospital. I've always said that I married Lynette because she would be the mother to my kids my mother wasn't to me: present, not high and locked in a room chanting her mantra, "Freak out!"—and generally concerned with her children's well-being. I didn't anticipate that she'd be wildly overconcerned with her children's well-being. You've heard of "helicopter moms"?

She's Airwolf ( ⌕ Google It ) **bit.ly/ESA-Airwolf.** I'm more of a "submarine dad." You don't even know I'm there.

I might not mind the worry so much if there was consistency. Lynette, being a female, suffers from what I have termed "chick-think," a disease that has mutated and spread to many men in our society. It's the inability to grasp problems with rationality and to approach them based on facts rather than feelings. The story that encapsulates the unscientific method is a tale of two waters.

When my kids were still young, they toddled around a large house in the Hollywood Hills. This house had a courtyard off the kitchen, and off that courtyard was access to a side gate. On the other side of said gate was a nine-foot-deep swimming pool (next to an underground bar that I built myself, called Ace in the Hole, featuring portholes that looked into the pool). While you could see whoever was swimming in the pool from the bar, you could not see the gate to the pool from the kitchen. This is where Lynette and I had an epic argument about water. I noticed that the gardener would pass through that gate and always leave it unlatched. Not wanting to come home to find my twins in Davy Jones's locker, I told him to make sure to latch it every time. And then I told him to latch it every time. And then I told him to latch it every time. I could write that sentence ten more times, but rather than annoy you with the actual quantity of conversations in which I had to insist that he not facilitate the drowning of my children, I'll just let the record show that until I started docking him fifty dollars for each time I found it unlatched, this behavior persisted. It happened only once after that, which should tell you socialist fucksticks out there all you need to know about capitalism and incentive.

Anyway, knowing that this gardener was too lazy or stupid to do what I wanted, or that he had a vendetta against my two-year-olds, I told Lynette that she needed to check the gate after he left. Her response was something to the effect of: "The gardener left the gate open. That's what he does." I agreed and insisted, "That's why, when he leaves, you've got to check it." She responded, "But he left it open." I said what I always say: "He's dumb. We're not." If you ever hear me say that, just assume I'm calling you dumb.

Juxtapose this with the time shortly thereafter when she asked me to refill one of the twins' sippy cups. When I went to replenish it with tap water, she slapped it out of my hand like I was filling it with water from Fukushima. She practically dove on me in slow motion, shouting, *"Noooooo!!!"* like a Secret Service agent taking a bullet for the president. Tons of energy to make sure the kids don't end up with a cup of municipal water in their belly, but very little to make sure they don't end up on a coroner's slab with pool water in their lungs.

Here's another quick water-related illustration of chick-think and how it permeates my life and every facet of society. Lynette spends my money on veggie wash. This is a useless spray bottle to clean your vegetables of pesticides, dirt, and wax while simultaneously cleaning your wallet of seven dollars. There's no way this shit works any better than what comes out of our spigot. You know how I know? (Here comes the confession, Lynette. Please turn this page. In fact, you should probably skip the next twenty-two pages.) Every three months, when we start to run low, I top it off from the sink. I've been cutting it with tap water like a coke dealer steps on his product with baby laxatives. I'm happy to report that neither Sonny nor Natalia has died from E. coli or Roundup on their carrot sticks.

When Lynette reads that, she's probably going to murder me, so to the future homicide detective investigating my poisoning, the above paragraph is your motive. On that note...

## The True Crime Is True Crime

A few years back I was putzing around in the office while Lynette was out somewhere spending my money. Natalia came in with a friend who was over and said, "We want to go to Pinkberry." My house at the time was only a few blocks away. All she would need to do is stroll down the shady side of my street, walk half a block, pop out, and Pinkberry would be right there. My first thought was, *Good, I'll just give you twenty bucks and you can walk to get Froyo.* My second thought was, *I'll be crucified. The other kid's parents will find out, call Lynette, and I'll never hear the end of it.* Actually, that was my third thought. My second thought was, *This will buy me a half hour to hop on YouPorn.*

To avoid getting the frozen shoulder from Lynette, I walked with them to the frozen yogurt place—among the millions of things I've done that my parents never would've. Froyo didn't exist when I was a kid, but even if it had, it never would have passed these lips.

> (BTW) Is there any less necessary abbreviation than "Froyo"? Anyone who's talking about frozen yogurt isn't in a hurry. It's the least urgent of all foods. You eat it on lazy Saturday afternoons. You have all the time in the world to say both words if you're considering getting frozen yogurt. Guys rappelling out of helicopters aren't yelling, "I'll see you at the Froyo place."

Shrimp scampi needs an abbreviation, not frozen yogurt. There's never been a situation where someone says "Froyo" and yells *"stat!"*

Frozen yogurt places are the greatest scam in the world. They can pay a teen with bad skin to sell you a three-ounce medium or give you a wine barrel sawed in half and let you fill it yourself, because they know that no kid—or, sadly, any of the adults who act like kids—is going to know when to say when. They just let the hogs go to the trough. We also trick ourselves into thinking that it's healthy because it's yogurt. It's not. Especially after we put a wheelbarrow of gummy worms on top of it. It's like a slot machine that cums sugar into a cup. It's a one-armed bandit that leaves you with one leg from diabetes. 😬

When Lynette came home, I told her the story and she acted as if I had actually let them go. The fact that I had even considered it was a problem. I was getting the stink eye for something I hadn't done. To defend myself against my non-crime, I said, "This is a nice neighborhood." Lynette shot back, "That's exactly the type of neighborhoods they go to."

Where does she get this shit? I'll tell you. *Dateline* and all those other Friday-night "true crime" shows. These are heroin to Lynette. Whether it's about a mother killing her kids, like with the whole Casey Anthony trial, which Lynette didn't miss a second of, or *Making a Murderer*, the Netflix documentary about a random photographer for Autotrader who got murdered when she showed up to take the pictures, Lynette's all in. My wife could be an FBI profiler based on the amount of true crime she's studied. She definitely watches *Dateline* because their fear-mongering tagline is "Don't Watch Alone!" And she definitely tries to not watch alone.

Nope, she tries to get me in on it. My thought is, *Yeah, there're some really horrible people out there. I'm depressed enough with my life. I don't need to peek into another person's tragedy.*

These shows are loved by all women and their cuckolded husbands. They're catnip for the pussywhipped. I don't know and wouldn't want to know any guy who is into this shit. Henry Rollins is not watching *Dateline*. It's just not practical enough. These murders are solved. It's not like if you crack the case half-way through, you can call in and win a prize.

Chicks don't understand statistics. They watch this shit and think, *Well, there's a 50/50 chance that'll be me.* It plays into the victim mentality. Something could happen to you or your family. It's always inter-family. It's never "A Crip shot a Blood. The end." When a ferry overturns in the Indian Ocean, we don't even notice it, because we're not going to be on any Bengali boats anytime soon. But we're all going to let our kids walk to the park. It has to tickle the "That could be me" part of women. It has to pull the fear lever for them. "In a quiet neighborhood." "Wait, I'm in a quiet neighborhood." "It could happen anywhere." "Oh shit, we just bought a house anywhere!" We're days away from a promo that says, "On a special *48 Hours*. Look behind you!"

My beef with this is that we're teaching our kids to be victims, or potential victims. They're all walking around expecting to be abducted. As discussed in my last book, Natalia is not scared of zip lines and other daredevil stuff. She's wound up in the emergency room multiple times, and we've done more than one family whitewater rafting trip. During one of them, she jumped off a twenty-five-foot bridge to plunge into a forty-degree river fed by icy water coming off melting mountain snowpack. But a few years ago at the raceway in Fontana, I let Sonny go to the bathroom alone and got a ration of shit from Lynette. I let her know that less than 40 percent of vintage race guys are pedophiles. The next day Natalia joined us at the track, and at a certain point she had to pee. I told her and Sonny they could go together—Daddy was watching. She adamantly refused to go without me. After a long negotiation, I lost. She made me go and stand outside the ladies' room. What happened to little SHE-vel Knievel?

Natalia's absorbing all this shit. It's part of her environment. I walk into the bedroom at ten at night and there's Nancy Grace saying, "They tied up the father, rounded up the kids, locked them in the basement, and set the house ablaze. If it could happen in this tight-knit community, it could happen anywhere." And Lynette is all ears. If Mama is steeping in this stupidity, how can she not be passing it on to her daughter?

Lynette's current addiction is *Locked Up Abroad*, another fear-based "It could happen to you" show. We should lock up all the broads who are into *Locked Up Abroad*, because the constant ingestion of fear about shit that will never happen is ruining our society. Ninety percent of the women watching this have never left their state, never mind the country.

I can't blame just Lynette. This has seeped into our culture.

Around the time the twins were eight or nine, there was a story in the news about two kids in Silver Spring, Maryland. The boy was ten, and his little sister was six. The mother let them walk to a park a mile from their house. Alone. Guess what? They *were* abducted. Lynette and every other mother's fear had come true. Except they weren't snatched up by a creep with an air-brushed van. They were picked up by the police after someone with a vagina (sadly, that includes a lot of guys I know) spotted them walking alone and called the fuzz. They were taken in to child protective services. Oh, and this happened twice. After an "investigation," they were released back to the parents who had had the audacity to let the two kids walk alone.

What is more traumatizing, the nonexistent horror of an Astro van abduction or the actual damage done by being taken into custody by police, being interviewed by the Department of Children and Families, and not being able to call your parents to let them know where you are? When did everyone become a tattletale pussy? They were fine. When I was a kid, I would ride my Huffy unattended, unmolested, and unhydrated all day long in the San Fernando Valley with no supervision and no problems. This is a rite of passage. This is how kids know they are safe. They wander, they come back to their secure base, and they develop self-reliance and resilience. To the cunt who called the cops, please watch *Stand by Me* and shut the fuck up.

My wife and every other woman in America are now convinced that if their kids go to the boulevard alone, they'll end up as an amber alert. This never happens. It's always the disgruntled dad in a divorce gone wrong who takes them. Because of this crap, I'm likely to become a disgruntled dad in a divorce gone wrong. There was one case in 2016 when some nutjob tried to snatch a thirteen-year-old girl from a Dollar Store in Florida and the mom fought him off, but I'm convinced that there was a secret meeting of hysterical moms who paid the guy eighty-five dollars so that Nancy Grace could show the footage for three days and say, "It could happen anywhere, anytime." By the way, "It could happen anywhere" doesn't really apply in this case. A Dollar Store in Florida is where most weird shit goes down. It makes the evening news if someone *doesn't* attempt to abduct a teen at a Dade County Dollar Store.

The more Lynette absorbs this stuff, the tighter she clings to the kids. I'm afraid to ask her, "When is the right time for them to be able to leave the house alone?" I'm pretty sure the answer would be, "As soon as Natalia gets her brown belt in Brazilian jiu-jitsu and right after Sonny has prostate surgery."

Even the fictionalized versions play on fear. Last year when the NXIVM sex cult got busted, Lifetime execs immediately started turning it into a movie titled *NXIVM Cult: A Mother's Nightmare*. What I realized is that you can put "A Mother's Nightmare" after anything and turn it into a Lifetime movie. It could be about a crab boat sinking in the Bering Strait and if they put "A Mother's Nightmare" after it, every dumb chick would tune in. "I'm a mother. I have nightmares."

The only true-crime story that wouldn't qualify for this is *The Monica Lewinsky Story: A Father's Nightmare*.

Last year someone tweeted me a picture of their TV screen with the channel guide. Two spots above an episode of *Crank Yankers* was a Lifetime movie called *A Mother's Worst Fear*. It didn't even have a prefix like *The Brenda Goldstein Story*. They just cut right to the chase. Eventually, these shows are going to end up like the Coke cans with people's names on them. I think I could make some serious money on this idea. I'll get a list of the most popular names for mothers ages twenty-seven to forty-two and personalize the show names. Eight percent of the population must have common names like Michelle, Catherine, Christine, and so forth, so some chick named Jennifer will be scrolling through the channels and see *A Daughter Abducted: Jennifer's Worst Nightmare*, freak out, and watch it. Meanwhile the Ace Man will be laughing all the way to the bank. Next week would be the same exact movie swapped out with "Karen." Tell me this isn't a genius idea.

TV's goal is to scare dopey dames into watching. And it works. Why? Because they don't have problems. Twenty percent of our brain is wired to protect us, to watch out for predators, but white chicks in America have no natural predators, so they have to create them. You ever notice that these movies always star blonde white chicks? They don't market them to black mothers, because black mothers have real problems. They're keeping their kids out of gangs, hustling as single moms, working three jobs, and whatnot. And there's no Asian version of this, because Asians are all too busy working and becoming thoracic surgeons.

> ( BTW ) Before I move off TV and fear, I have to go on a quick little tangent about *Naked and Afraid*. Two thoughts: First, it's got to be weird to be a cameraman on that show, constantly walking around with a camera on your shoulder and a boner in your shorts. I guess as far as gigs go, it's either that or be on *Cops* chasing a junkie down an alley.
>
> Second, I'm really annoyed with my cable provider for trying to convince me to watch *Naked and Afraid*. Every time I go to my channel guide, there seems to be an ad for this show. I have a computer. I can watch a show called *Naked and Fucking*. That's a lot better than what the National Geographic channel is offering. I don't need to see scrambled tits and people covered in mud and bug bites. I'll call you when they cancel *Naked and Nineteen Years Old Getting Plowed by a Black Guy*. 😁

We have brainwashed our pussy-ass selves into thinking that everyone under a hundred pounds who is not tied down is going to be abducted by ISIS. My wife's greatest fear is that the kids will be alone, a van will pull up, and a great white shark will jump out. (Didn't see that one coming, did you?) Statistically, they are much more likely to die in a car accident, but that happens every day. We're not in El Salvador. Cartel abductions are not common practice in my neighborhood. If you want your kid in the hospital, let them Rollerblade. That will have them in the ER much faster than killer bees, encephalitis, E. coli, or whatever fear du jour the news is serving up.

## All the News That's Shit to Print

Once you become a famous, famous celebrity like me, and people start writing about you in the press, you'll notice just how incompetent reporters are. Like a quinceañera, bar mitzvah, or any other rite of passage, everyone should have a reporter follow them around and interview them for an article in the newspaper. Then sit back and watch how much stuff is inaccurate. When I was doing *Catch a Contractor* with husband-and-wife team Skip and Alison Bedell, *The Hollywood Reporter* referred to her as my wife. When the *Washington Post* did an article about my battle with the patent trolls, they said that I "settled" with the trolls when, in fact, we beat them. And, as I've railed about for years, *Entertainment Weekly* famously wrote an article about season five of *The Man Show* and said that Jimmy Kimmel was making "an ill-fated move into late night" and that Comedy Central had performed "a Carolla-ectomy." Nice work, dickwads. Comedy Central begged me to do season five, and I said no. We had so many meetings where they licked my balls trying to get me to come back that I eventually had to stop picking up the phone. (They were right about Kimmel, though. Whatever happened to that guy?)

That's print news. Now that I know they're incompetent boobs, I have sworn off reading. I have vowed to never read again. (Yeah, that's why.) Local television news, on the other hand, is a cluster-fuck. When they're not trying to gin up fear with stuff like "Germ Week," they're giving you "No shit, Sherlock" information. Every year we get treated to the same idiotic stories about how to "beat the heat." I would be much better served by a news story about how to beat my meat. The first of their groundbreaking ideas is to always "hydrate." Good tip. How about, "Try not to wrap yourself in tinfoil and eat Vaseline on your roof"? No joke, one actual tip I heard was, "It's hot, but not as hot if you don't stand in the sun." Thanks. My cat figured that out. I'm an adult man, and you're telling me to stand in the shade?

> **BTW** In L.A. we're consistently treated to the news spectacle of the high-speed chase. Once I heard a reporter say the car was being driven by "a possible gang member." Everyone driving a car in the San Fernando Valley is a possible gang member. We know it's not a Jehovah's Witness. Reporters cover those things long enough that when they eventually head down the side street in the shitty neighborhood, idiots come out to wave at the car and the news helicopter. This prompted another of my brilliant sting operation ideas. We stage a high-speed chase. We get an excellent stunt driver, like Tanner Foust, behind the wheel of a drug lord's confiscated car and have the cops follow him. Then everyone who comes out to high-five him and throw stuff at the cop cars gets arrested. You know they've got a couple of outstanding warrants.

I used to think the news just reported the news. I would look at the *L.A. Times* growing up and see a story about an accident with a minivan and two fatalities. Now we've veered into this sensationalistic, emotion-driven, chick-catering news. It's no longer, "There was a two-car collision on Pico and Venice that left two dead. LAPD believe alcohol was a factor." Instead, we have chicks and soft dudes saying, "There was a car accident involving a child. *A child*. She loved *My Little Pony*. She'll never see her eighteenth birthday. She'll never vote!" Ugh, shut the fuck up and spit the facts out.

Speaking of the *L.A. Times*, it's a worthless rag that makes me glad I'm functionally illiterate. They had an op-ed after the Parkland shooting that made *me* want to go on a killing spree. Let me preface all of this with the fact that, while you can yank me *and* you can crank me, I'm no Ted Nugent. I own guns for protection, but I'm not a gun nut—though I once saw a documentary called *Red Dawn*, so I think I'm well qualified to speak about violence in schools.

After the Parkland shooting, the *L.A. Times* editorial board wrote the following:

> *We listen to the bleatings of the gun enthusiasts that, well, if those teachers had guns, then this wouldn't have been as bad. Been as bad. Think about that. If a pistol-strapping chemistry teacher had grabbed her .45 and unloaded on today's gunman after he killed, what, one student? Three? Five? That would be good news?*

Of course it would be good news, you fucking imbeciles. If you were student number six who didn't die because some adult was armed, that would be very fucking good news. Whoever wrote this is an insane person. I was the worst student at North Hollywood High. If I was part of the *L.A. Times* editorial team,

I'd have stood up in that meeting and said, "Hey fucksticks, we're shitting on our own point." In their attempt to make the case against guns, they made a very compelling argument for arming teachers. They must have been amazing in speech and debate club in high school.

If this were a news story about a school bus crash instead of a school shooting, and someone was able to stop all but one kid on the bus from being killed, that would be good news. You'd be touting that person as a hero.

We get it, *L.A. Times* editorial team, you hate guns. Do I want to live in a world where armed teachers are necessary? Fuck no. But I don't want to live in a world with Kim Jong Un, the Taliban, or DJ Khaled either. We must, as Dr. Drew has always said, "accept reality on reality's terms." Even the loved ones of those killed would understand that. If you gathered all the family members of every kid who died in a school shooting and conducted the world's most uncomfortable survey asking, "Would you have preferred a teacher at the school be armed?" all of their hands would go up. How could they not?

Your editorial is the opposite of sense. If that pistol-strapping chemistry teacher was a good shot and could put one between the Parkland shooter's eyes before he killed again, you'd be a fool not to want that. By pushing this agenda and stoking the fire against this common-sense measure, you are now partially responsible. Please write a story about yourself as an accessory to murder.

If every kid who wanted to go into a school and rack up a body count thought there was someone there armed and trained, that would slow their roll. Significantly. Don't try to convince me otherwise. They know that schools, just like movie theaters and country music concerts, are soft targets. The dipshits at the

*L.A. Times* are hoping to keep schools soft, just like their brains. I wish we knew specifically who the author of the editorial is so we could never listen to anything they said ever again.

If it's not outright stupidity, like at the *L.A. Times*, it's shoddy reporting and exaggeration. Do you remember the stories about pedophiles taking advantage of the kids in cages at the border? How true did that turn out to be? It was a complete mischaracterization by a Democratic congressman, but the news media ran with it until the Office of Refugee Resettlement rightfully pushed back. The real version is bad enough. You don't need to gild the lily. (We need a better metaphor, since those are both good things. Pissing on the train wreck? I'll get back to you.) What this achieves is tune-out. News, you're the boy who cried wolf.

( BTW ) Speaking of news and wolf, how bummed must Wolf Blitzer be with the decline of news? He rose to prominence with grand orchestral music swelling underneath him while he reported on Desert Storm. Now he's got teen-girl techno blaring beneath him while he reports on Stormy Daniels. 😁

I started tuning out when I heard all the stories of the roving gangs raping and pillaging at the Superdome during Hurricane Katrina. Of course, none of that turned out to be true either. The reports made it seem like *The Purge*, but it turned out a total of six people died. Four of the deaths were natural, one was a suicide, and one was a drug overdose. None of the people were bludgeoned to death on the fifty-yard line. It's a confined area. It's not like there's a lot of ground to cover. It's an acre. If you can't truthfully report what's going on in a space that Terry Bradshaw can cover accurately during football season, you're fucking useless as a journalist.

One of the problems is that for every bias you have, there's a network to reinforce it. Think Hillary Clinton is the devil in a blue pantsuit and want to hear about it from a hot blonde? Might I interest you in some Fox News? Think Trump is Hitler and want to hear about it from a person of color who is either gay or transitioning? One order of MSNBC coming up.

A quick Fox-related side story. I wasn't joking about the hot blondes. Greta Van Susteren was a Fox News star but you don't see her anymore because they apparently instituted a "7UP" policy—no chick can grace their airwaves unless they are a seven or higher. I did a *Fox and Friends*–type show a couple years ago called *Outnumbered*. It was aptly named, because I was definitely outnumbered, surrounded by blonde chicks with the whitest teeth you can imagine. There should be a dental office called Fox Chix that just advertises that they do the teeth of all the Fox News Barbie dolls. The only thing whiter than a Fox News chick's teeth is her audience.

At a certain point I just blurted out, "Who do you think has slept together less, Bill and Hillary Clinton or Oprah and Stedman?" They were shocked. I put it to you, dear reader. Who do you think has boned less? ( ⊙ Google It ) **bit.ly/ESA-Poll**

The point is, the networks do not work because they don't have to. They've got their audience. Now, all they have to do is keep them. Fox isn't competing with CNN, because anyone who watches Fox thinks CNN is liberal propaganda, and anyone who watches CNN thinks Fox is state-run television for "dear leader" Donald. Actual reporting goes by the wayside, while ginning up resentment and anger at the other team takes precedent. Facts be damned.

Take the case of Nick Sandmann, the kid who supposedly taunted the Native American elder on the steps of the Lincoln Memorial. That story was basically made in a lab to get liberals pissed. He was white, male, and Catholic; his family had money; and he was wearing a MAGA hat. It's like when you bait a mouse-trap: you put a little peanut butter on it because it's their favorite. This was the perfect bait for the media.

We all saw that, but virtually no one saw the video of an eighty-five-year-old man having a prayer vigil in front of a Planned Parenthood in San Francisco. Not ringing a bell? Hmmm. I wonder why? You should definitely remember it, because a "woke" San Francisco guy went up to him and yanked a pro-Jesus sign out of his hands. When the elderly man tried to hang on to his sign, the younger guy knocked him to the ground and started kicking him. You can even hear him on tape saying, "Stay down, old man, unless you want to get hurt." This guy is the worst person in the world. I'm pro-choice too, but I don't feel compelled to curb-stomp the elderly if they disagree.

I don't feel that this is "news" either—it's just footage of a crime—but if the smirking kid staring down the Indian is "news," then this definitely is. The point is, you didn't know anything about it because it doesn't check the right boxes. Sure, it's some-one young versus someone old and this one is more violent, so it should have been seen and shared more widely. But in this case, the old man isn't a "marginalized" person and is pro-life, so it didn't make the cut at MSNBC.

The most insidious narrative that the more liberal networks propagate is about race. I accept that they are idiots playing on our emotions. But I do not accept their agenda to convince everyone, especially people of color, that they have a target on their back.

There's a general trend in the media (except on Fox News) to prove that this is an irreparably racist nation in which hate crimes occur every day. And comparing it to some magical land in your head that doesn't exist, holding it to some impossible standard, doesn't help. If America were a quarterback in the NFL, these assholes would declare, "Every incomplete pass is unacceptable. I have zero tolerance for incompletions," rather than focus on his 70 percent completion rate.

Immediately after 9/11, there were violent attacks on Muslims. Sadly, there was also violence toward Sikhs, who aren't Muslim, but rednecks thought they were because they wear turbans. But if you think about other cultures, or even about our culture in a different time period, how much different do you think the reaction would have been? We didn't go total Kristallnacht. Other countries, even in the present day, would be having a full ethnic cleansing if 9/11 had happened on their soil. Fortunately, many of those shithole nations don't have a building that tops three stories or a plane that isn't currently being pulled by a donkey.

After the 2016 election, *USA Today* sifted through over 3,500 Russian Facebook posts that were designed to create chaos in our system. The narrative on the news is that the Russians were trying to get Trump elected. While that may be partially true, what they were really trying to do was sow division. And, boy, did they find a way to do it. It wasn't about trashing one candidate over the other. Only one hundred of the ads even mentioned Clinton or Trump. More than half of the posts (55 percent) were about race. They saw this as our weakness and exploited it. Let me make that point again, this time in all caps. They saw this as OUR WEAKNESS. They knew they could shake up our bees nest because we're so primed and ready to attack each other around race. And a lot of that blame falls squarely on the news media.

Somewhere during the Obama presidency, racist cop stories became fashionable. Just like the shark attack stories, pit bull stories, and road rage stories. The news grabs on to trends and makes it seem like this shit happens every day. Why? Because you watched last night and they want you to watch tonight. Once we stop taking the anxiety bait, the news moves on to something else.

It plays not just on fear but also on thinly veiled narcissism. We human beings need something attacking us. We have the same caveman wiring that protected us for millennia from predators and warring tribes. We need an enemy to satisfy that part of our brains. To give *us* a sense of identity, we need a *them*. The Hatfields have the McCoys, Sunnis have Shiites, and the Harlem Globetrotters have those robots on *Gilligan's Island*. Whitey's version of this is Purell and veggie wash. Black people's version of this is Trump and racist cops.

I'm not trying to make the case that there are no hate crimes or racist cops in this country. There are. I'm just saying let's get it right, because every Chicken Little false alarm damages us as a culture. A certain percentage of people will never hear the retraction, if there even is one, and thus will continue to deepen their paranoia about the cops, the president, and society in general. When people feel victimized, they often act out with aggression, thinking, *Let's get them before they get us.* And if they don't act out, they act *in* with depression. The worst thing you can do to a person is convince them they are a victim.

The old newsroom saying is, "If it bleeds, it leads." Well, they've got that blood on their hands. All the "hate speech" that gets liberals riled up on campuses and the internet amounts to nothing. But the speech I hate, which is "You all have a target on your back," does get people killed. When politicians and other grifters preach to the black masses that every cop is out to kill them, a certain percentage are going to absorb that and start treating cops like the enemy, either by running from them, fighting them, or disrespecting them. This is a fantastic way to get shot. The new trend at the time of the writing of this book is dumping buckets of water on cops in Harlem. This is the breakdown of the rule of law right before our eyes. Guess what happens? Cops decide they don't want to be part of an involuntary ice bucket challenge, they stop going into these shitty neighborhoods, and crime goes up.

There's a lot of talk nowadays about white privilege. You know what white privilege is? Not having to join a group and feel like I have to think like everyone else in the group and drink the victim Kool-Aid. My white privilege is knowing that cops generally tend to be insane assholes and not racists out to get me.

My *Reasonable Doubt* cohost, Mark Geragos, represented the widow of Daniel Shaver, an unarmed twenty-six-year-old man who was shot and killed by a white police officer in Mesa, Arizona. The officer was later acquitted despite video evidence. I'm sure you all saw that body-camera footage.

Oh, wait. You didn't. Because Shaver was white. If he wasn't, MSNBC would be showing it nonstop, because it was by far the worst police killing ever. A citizen called the Mesa Police Department saying they saw someone in a hotel room with a gun. It later turned out that Shaver was an exterminator and had an Airsoft pellet gun for shooting rodents. For clarity, I don't blame the person who called it in. I blame Officer Philip Brailsford, along with Sergeant Charles Langley—Brailsford's superior on the scene, who shouted confusing orders and did the exact opposite of de-escalation. After being ordered from his room and into the hallway, this poor bastard was told to lie on his stomach. Sobbing and begging for his life, saying, "Please don't shoot me," Shaver, who was drunk at the time, reached to pull his shorts up because they had slipped after he was ordered to crawl on the floor of the La Quinta. Trigger-happy, Brailsford unloaded five shots into Shaver's back, chest, and head, killing him. This wasn't an "officer-involved shooting" or "a tragic mistake" like what sometimes gets talked about on the news. This was an execution. Despite this, Brailsford was acquitted and reinstated to the department in August 2018, and was promptly granted "retirement" on medical grounds, receiving his full pension. If Shaver had been black, Arizona would be on fire like Ferguson. But it didn't fit the news narrative.

Oh, and did I mention that Brailsford had "You're Fucked" inscribed on the stock of his AR-15? Because one thing we can all agree on is that almost all cops are assholes. That profession attracts a certain breed of cat, the kind that likes power and is ready to wield it. They don't get into that line of work to hassle and potentially kill *black* people, just people. It doesn't matter whether the people are African American motorists giving them lip or a drunk pest-control guy with a BB gun. Look at how cops outfit themselves nowadays. Every officer looks like he's hanging off a Humvee in Fallujah. Robocop had less technology on him than your average cop does today, and there are guys jousting at Medieval Times wearing less armor. But the more we focus on their being racists, the less we focus on them turning into the Terminator.

> (BTW) I see a lot of fat cops out there. Much like my idea that for every hundred dollars spent over a thousand-dollar base-line, the bride must be able to fit into her wedding dress for one year, I think all cops should be issued one, and only one, vest on their first day after graduating the academy. If they eat

too many tacos over the years hiding in their patrol car with a radar gun handing out chickenshit tickets, and their gut starts slopping out of their Kevlar vest, that's just more to get shot at. I think this will motivate them to get out and walk the beat a little bit more.

So how about we stop with the stories about how it's open season on black people for racist white cops and talk about the real thing killing young black men—other young black men? No. That would be part of the "honest dialogue" that everyone is always asking for but runs from when some intellectually honest person like myself brings up the crisis of fatherhood in the black community.

You know who certainly won't do it? The so-called community leaders, one of whom has plied his trade of race-hustling so well, he's found his way to MSNBC—Al Sharpton. Al's feelings about the Jews are far more racist than anything Donald Trump has ever said about black people. (At least in public. How many N-bombs get dropped in the clubhouse after Tiger Woods beats him at Mar-a-Lago, I can only speculate.) You've got to go digging into Al's early work, like Tawana Brawly and Crown Heights, to fully appreciate what a bag of shit this guy is.

There's nothing about him that is even vaguely religious other than his self-applied title "Reverend." Can you imagine a white version of Al Sharpton? That would be like me saying, "I believe Joey Buttafuoco speaks for me as a member of the white community. We should give him a show on CNN."

Al comes to your town, but unlike Grand Funk Railroad, he's not there to help you party down. He's there to shake you down.

Al's going to threaten to boycott your business until you cut him a check and he goes home.

There is one thing I do miss about the old Al Sharpton, though. Actually it's about 150 things, namely pounds. I want Al to get fat again. I miss the Al Sharpton of the '80s, who got the hot comb out and wore a medallion outside of a velour running suit. It was like he got a medal at the Fat Olympics in the hundred-meter waddle. ( Google It ) **bit.ly/ESA-Sharpton**

Whether it's Al Sharpton, Maxine Waters, Don King, Cornel West, Jesse Jackson, or any number of white politicians hoping to get or keep the black vote, they are profiting from the false narrative that we live in a racist society and that anyone who's ever purchased a Jimmy Buffett, Dave Matthews, or Kenny Chesney album is out to kill black people. As the social philosopher and writer Eric Hoffer said, "Every great cause begins as a movement, becomes a business, and eventually degenerates into a racket."

Since we'll never have an actual honest dialogue on race, I hope you've enjoyed my honest monologue.

## Victim or Asshole?

Before I close out this chapter I'd like to share a list of people who have taken one thing and built their whole life around it, whether it's something that makes them a victim or just makes them an asshole. If you're one of them, prepare to be triggered.

> **Fake-Cough Guy:** Not too long ago, this happened to one of my lackeys when he was smoking a cigarette on the sidewalk in Burbank outside a comedy club where we'd just finished a live podcast. Some hipster dude walked by my staffer blowing a butt and did an over-the-top fake hacking cough as if he'd

taken in a lungful of secondhand smoke, thus making him a firsthand pussy. In my world, I have no problem with that person being taken out in a terrorist attack. How long is that guy's day? Every bus he walks by, every leaf blower, does he have to do the fake cough?

The only proper response to that individual is the one I shouted when it happened to me some years ago at three a.m. in front of the CBS Radio building after Dr. Drew and I had finished doing *Loveline*: "Shut the fuck up, pussy." We get it, you think smoking is bad and want to shame me for it, so you need to act like I tied you to a chair and blew a carton's worth of Marlboro Red smoke in your face. Walk to the other side of the street, hold your breath as you walk past, or just deal with it. But no, that wouldn't make you a victim. As I said, have a "Fuck you," "Fuck off," "Shut the fuck up," "Go fuck yourself," or any of the fine family of "fuck" phrases chambered and ready to go. And have no fear of retaliation; you can definitely kick that guy's ass. It's not like Chuck Liddell and Brock Lesnar are walking around doing the fake cough because you had the audacity to light up.

**"What Happened?" Guy:** This guy drives me nuts. This is the person who sees your shattered smartphone screen and needs to know how it happened. He sees a cracked screen and he's gonna crack the case. What answer other than "I dropped it" is there? Am I supposed to reply, "Mountain lion. Fended it off with my Samsung Galaxy." When there's a tale that involves a sniper's bullet, I'll tell you, but until then assume it slipped out of my sweatpants pocket in the Ralph's parking lot and cease your CSI—Cracked Screen Investigation.

It goes back to the victimhood thing. This guy wants to call attention to your misfortune or mistake so that you can join him in feeling like an unlucky, downtrodden person. Is this going to be endlessly fascinating for him, or is it just schadenfreude? What information can he glean from this that makes his life better? None, so if this is you, move on or I'm going to use my cracked iPhone to delete your contact and never speak to you again.

**Doesn't Like Barbecue Guy:** To be clear, this isn't a vegan or a vegetarian. Those pussies don't hate barbecue; they hate their abusive stepdads. I'm talking about a person who does eat meat but still isn't into firing up the grill. Barbecue is an indicator: Are you into life or not? If I ask someone, "Do you like barbecue?" and they do twenty minutes on baby-back versus beef ribs, they're in. This guy also enjoys travel, scotch, and 69ing. You know, all the important things in life. He knows how to carpe the fuck out of the diem. No one has ever said, "I don't like barbecuing because it gets in the way of my dirt track oval racing on my Harley." Barbecue is messy and it takes hours to prep, but it's worth it. Enjoying working the grill shows good character. And it's communal. No one eats barbecue alone. Unlike as in the most nonsensical book title ever.
( Q Google It ) **bit.ly/ESA-Brenner**

The only guy I can't have barbecue with is the one who wears the apron while shirtless and working the grill. He's cut and he knows it. He's got a thirty-inch waist, and his lats are sticking out from behind the apron. He's playing like he doesn't have time for the T-shirt, he's gonna get back in the pool soon, as if that eleven seconds is going to make a difference. The apron over your washboard abs may say "Kiss the

Cook," but I say the cook can kiss my ass. As you can tell, I hate guys who have to show off that they're in shape. Which leads to...

**Separate-Toes-Shoe Guy:** This jack-off needs you to think he's going to bust out into a sprint at any moment. He's in the middle of a marathon and just had to stop into Albertsons for some paper towels. He's the same guy who has the watch that's good up to seven thousand feet underwater. Is he planning on doing some free diving wearing his watch after he leaves the Chipotle in Arleta, or is he just showing off? He thinks his shoes say "I'm athletic," but they really say "I'm ass-letic." Put on some Skechers like a normal person. You're not Zola Budd.
( Q Google It ) **bit.ly/ESA-Zola**

**Slip-On-Vans Dad:** Speaking of footwear, there are certain shoes that go with certain types of people. Old comedy writers are always in New Balance. I've been in a million writers' rooms with a million middle-aged Jewish guys, and they were all wearing New Balance. I guarantee that Larry David is wearing a pair of New Balance shoes right now. They shouldn't be called New Balance; they should be called Jew Balance. Well, Vans are the customary footwear of the hipster dad. He drives the vintage Bronco, he has funky frames on his glasses, and he's got the black-and-white checkerboard slip-on Vans. He's too cool for laces. I don't like it when dudes in their fifties are wearing the same shoes Spicoli wore in *Fast Times at Ridgemont High*. Vans are neither fish nor fowl when it comes to footwear. They're not good for running, but they're not dressy either. They're just slabs of vulcanized rubber with cloth around them. No one has ever done anything athletic in Vans except run from someone who wasn't in Vans.

**Work-Out Couple:** They're both fit, but fit for fifty-two. The guy is hanging on to the last remaining shreds of his youth, and she's got an eating disorder. They're both intense and in love and showing a little too much skin. I suspect this is foreplay. They go to the gym together, get the adrenaline going after a good pump, and then go home and have a good hump. There is an envy element to my hatred of this pairing. There's no way Lynette would be at the gym spotting for me and helping me with my form.

This is the healthy version of the other couple I can't stand, who sit on the same side of the diner booth. They love each other so much, they have to sidle up next to each other on the Naugahyde and bump elbows while eating corned beef hash. Again, it's shaming. No way Lynette and I are in a diner booth and not across from each other staring at our phones. I have a rule for the diner-booth couple. You're making it uncomfortable for me and other guys who can't stand to be that close to our wives with clothes on. If you insist on sitting next to your old lady while waiting for your eggs Benedict, you need to check your watch every eleven minutes and say, "Where are those guys?" so I can feel better.

**Steampunk Guy:** As far as I can tell, steampunk is punk with an engineering degree. This is rockabilly for people who make more than thirty-seven thousand dollars a year. This is the asshole who simultaneously dresses old-timey and futuristic, like what Jules Verne imagined someone in the future would look like. He's got the top hat that the lead lesbian from 4 Non Blondes wore and Red Baron goggles, which makes no sense. No one has ever needed aviator goggles and a top hat at the same time. If you're going fast enough that you need protective eyewear, your top hat is going to be gone with the wind. From the neck down, you're dressed like you're in a Paul Revere & the Raiders cover band, ( Q Google It ) **bit.ly/ESA-Revere** and from the neck up you look like Abe Lincoln. You go to conventions with other like-minded gents who have made fake dirigibles in their moms' basements out of PVC pipe and brass spray paint. Imagine a time traveler from 1781 who somehow got zapped into 2020 landing at a steampunk convention in Portland. He'd be so confused, he'd shit his pantaloons.

**Guy Who "Represents the 818" (or Any Other Shitty Area Code):** He was randomly born into this area code but has chosen to make an identity out of it. No one in Pacific Palisades or Malibu does this. James Brolin and Barbra Streisand aren't rocking tattoos showing that they represent the 310.

Having been through every inch of Southern California in my life, I can tell you that most of the parts represented by the 818 area code are shitholes. I've never been more depressed than when I had to work in Corona for two Saturdays while filming *Catch a Contractor*. It was like a dump truck full of Mexicans and garbage overturned at ninety miles an hour and just spread everywhere. It was broken couches on dirt lawns as far as the eye could see. The city crest for Corona is an abandoned shopping cart, a Camry with a space-saver spare, a leaf blower, and a pallet that's being used as a fence.

There're lots of towns in SoCal that have nice-sounding names, like Corona, that are third world. Diamond Bar sounds classy—at least it would be a decent name for a casino—but if you live there, you came up snake eyes. Lawndale sounds lush and green, but it's dusty and brown, and so are its citizens. The top of the list is Hawaiian Gardens. Hawaii? Sounds tropical.

Gardens? Sounds peaceful. Except if you live in Hawaiian Gardens, you know that you'd be better off living in an Al Qaeda training camp. You want to see the type of folk who live in Hawaiian Gardens? It's not a lovely hula dancer. It's this guy in this actual mugshot.

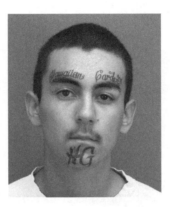

If I were in charge, these cities would be stripped of their names. There would just be a ranking system, and I'd make them compete to move up the list. Hawaiian Gardens, you're #238. You want to move up the list, clean up the gangs and the potholes and maybe you can overtake #237, formerly known as Palmdale.

**Doesn't Know How to Cut Pie Guy:** We all have one of these assholes at the office. Inevitably there is some staff meeting around Thanksgiving time, and someone brings in a home-made pumpkin pie and this dickhead cuts a trapezoid out of the center. It's a pie. Are you unaware of how pie works? There's no such thing as a lemon bar graph, but there is a pie chart. They're in color on every page of *USA Today*. Check them out.

You can always tell it's going to be a disaster, because this guy uses unconventional utensils. He's grabs a wooden spoon and he's ready to desecrate the true symbol of America, the apple pie. I'd rather you burn the flag than carve out anything other than a triangle from my pie. When the Jeffersons sang about finally getting a piece of the pie, they weren't talking about something the shape of Idaho cut out with a shoehorn.

**Lottery "System" Guy:** Any loser who plays the lottery deserves a righteous ass-kicking, but I feel a particular ire for the ones who think they "have a system." The lottery is, by its nature, random. You can't systematize something that is not systematizable. They're like, "First I take Bob Crane's birthday—he was born 7-13-28—then I add my current weight..." You understand this is not a system, right? Those are just random numbers.

And how's it going? Is this a theory you put together while living in your Chevette? You're chain-smoking at Binion's and arguing with a cocktail waitress over a two-for-one coupon. You have the same "system" for betting college football, but you're down nine hundred dollars for the year. The system you should really be working on is one to reestablish communication with your estranged adult daughter.

**Jeep-with-No-Doors Guy:** So the wisp of nylon on a coat hanger frame is too much? The implication with this is, "I've got to move quickly and be able to hop out with my husky." This guy thinks he's MacGyver or some sort of first responder, but the one I saw recently was pulling into a Round Table Pizza. I'd never stop watching a montage of these guys hopping out of their door-free cars and dropping their cell phones out of their pockets. To add insult to injury, the guy I saw also had a bumper sticker that said, "Got Soccer?"—which made me want to take my car with doors and ram him. These guys look at doorless driving as if they are emancipated million-aire minors on their twenty-first birthday. It's an adventure. It's freedom, baby. But when you really think about it, imagine the horror of driving any other car with no doors. It would be the opposite of liberating. It would be terrifying.

Picture going down the freeway at seventy-five miles per hour in your daily driver. If I pulled all the hinge pins and made you drive to work without doors on your Honda CRV, you would be freaked the fuck out. If you opened your door and a truck drove by and took it off and you had to drive to the auto body place two miles away, you would take side streets and crawl there. No other car works that way. That's how I know this Jeep creep isn't having a pleasurable experience. He's just advertising to the neighborhood that he's cooler than you.

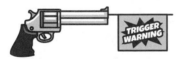

In closing, please understand this: Being a victim isn't a virtue. Being a victim has become valuable in our current fucked-up culture. If you are told to put your tit away because you're breast-feeding in public, you get to be a victim and blog about it until that kid is in college. But, like all currency, we've started seeing that currency getting counterfeited. Look no further than the whole Jussie Smollett situation.

I'm not suggesting that there are no victims in this world. I'm just sick of the media, politicians, and lawyers trying to convince everyone that they are one, because it's that mindset that will fuck you up more than any real victimization. I have never met a successful victim. We don't let people with physical disabilities convince themselves they're victims. We rally around them and cheer them on as they overcome actual adversity. We use footage of them with prosthetic arms and legs finishing marathons and climbing mountains. Guys whose legs were taken out by IEDs in Iraq are competing in the X Games, and we're all applauding. But if you're a "victim" of racism, or sexism, or homophobia, you get to be a victim for life and wear it like a badge instead of moving the fuck on like those other actual heroes.

In this country, victims can succeed. In fact, victims come to this country *to* succeed. The Jews and the Armenians came to America to escape victimization and become successful. The fucking Pilgrims came here to escape persecution. It's what this country was founded upon. But people who *view* themselves as victims cannot succeed. I resent that when I bring this topic up, I'm labeled a victim-blamer. No, I'm trying to help them and, in turn, us.

My friend Dennis Prager does a segment on his show every Friday called "The Happiness Hour," about how inflicting your bad mood on other people is selfish, and about how happiness is an achievement to be pursued because it improves our society. Nothing in our culture today—not politics, not mass media or social media—facilitates happiness. It all does the opposite. It actively tries to bum people out, to create fear, envy, paranoia, and hysteria.

To all of you out there who think you're fighting victimization by convincing everyone that they are victims, or potential victims, take a look in the mirror and punch yourself in the face. The victimizer you seek to fight is you.

# Chapter 4

## Commercial Grade

Nothing tells you where a culture is at more than its ads. Unlike everyone else, I don't fast-forward through commercials. I've always watched them. When I was a kid, they were considered full-fledged programming. We'd go to school and quote taglines like, "That's a spicy meat-a-ball," or "I can't believe I ate the whole thing." I remember seeing Wells Fargo ads with the stagecoach traveling through the Old West. It would be like, "Hey, there's something moving in front of me, and it's not a cockroach. Amazing!" Everybody had their version of the local car dealer who made crazy ads. Mine was Cal Worthington. He was a cowboy and had such a thick accent, he'd pronounce "Celica" SEE-lica. He'd wing-walk, strap himself to a plane doing a barrel roll, ride a hippo, or have a Bengal tiger jump on top of the car and bottom out the suspension. He sold used Chevy Novas in the San Fernando Valley, but he put more stunt work into his ads than Hal Needham. This was the closest I got to the circus in my childhood. ( Google It ) **bit.ly/ ESA-Needham**

Now, Madison Avenue is a feel-good factory cranking out ads catering to millennials to show how "woke" a corporation is, as if a corporation has feelings about anything other than the bottom line. Long gone are the *Mad Men* days, when ads shaped the culture and reflected the scotch-drenched dreams of guys slapping their secretaries on the ass. Pinstriped suits and porkpie hats have given way to board shorts and man buns, and you can see how our advertising age follows the trends, catering to the sensitivities of our rapidly pussifying culture. You need look no further than the ads from my childhood versus those airing today to see just how far we've fallen.

## Where Are the Ads of Old?

The granddaddy of them all was the Yuban coffee commercial, parodied so well in *Airplane!*, in which a couple is leaving a dinner party when the host appears and offers them a second cup of coffee. The husband, Jim, takes it. The wife, dejected and shamed, hangs her head like a dog that just got caught shitting on the carpet as we hear her internal monologue: "Jim never has a second cup of my coffee." Her credentials as an adequate wife were just torched. This is the female equivalent of being cuckolded. She was cuckolded by coffee.

This in no way, shape, or form mirrors my life at home. I'm typically the first one up brewing the coffee. And there is zero concern on Lynnette's part when she makes coffee as to whether I enjoy it. A more typical interaction is, Lynette and the kids return home from In-N-Out Burger, and when I ask what they brought me, there's the reply, "Did you want something?"

Then there were the Pledge commercials featuring the mother-in-law showing up unexpectedly. She'd pull out a white glove, drag her finger along the casing of the door frame, and shame the wife for the amount of dust on it. Then she'd pull an aerosol can of Pledge out of her purse and start dusting. We don't have that anymore. When I was ten I thought, *Oh, this is what I have to look forward to. This is what marriage is.* Bullshit. If I ever found Pledge in Lynette's purse, I would have to call Dr. Drew, because I'd think she was huffing it. That would be the only possible explanation. I'd be like, "Drew. Lynette's got a problem. Get the crew; we're having an intervention. She's huffing Endust. I should have known. She farted the other day, and it smelled like lemon."

Whether it was in ads or sitcoms, women used to be doing stuff when men got home from a hard day at the office. They'd be wearing yellow rubber gloves and a schmata while cleaning the oven. I wish we could get back to that. Lynette wouldn't even need to be cleaning the oven when I return from a full day of recording podcasts and writing. She could be on her laptop looking at *US Weekly*, but I would still love her to be wearing elbow-length yellow rubber gloves.

Or there are the Old Spice ads from my youth. Despite being from the same year as *Saturday Night Fever*, the sailors are getting off *Old Ironsides*. It was 1977, not 1877. For some reason, this guy is getting off *The Amistad* instead of a crab boat. Anyway, the narration says, "For centuries women have been waiting patiently for their men to return from sea" as the commercial shows a wife waiting in a lighthouse, hoping the tide would return her man and that he hadn't sunk to the bottom of the briny deep. For some reason, he steps off the ship clean-shaven. I feel like after a fortnight "on the crab," you're not going to come home with the best hygiene. And you're definitely going to nick your face up pretty badly trying to shave as waves rock your vessel.

The point is that Lynette's not waiting for me when I return from a long voyage. She's not at the rail of a lighthouse scanning the horizon for my return. When my car pulls up after I've been on the road doing stand-up all weekend, she lets out a disappointed sigh that it's me and not Grubhub.

> ( BTW ) There're a lot of great "rambling" songs about life on the road and fucking underage groupies—"Babe I'm Gonna Leave You," "We're an American Band," "Ramblin' Gamblin' Man." Songs used to declare from the jump that the singer wasn't about to be tied down. These Old Spice commercials remind me of the ultimate rambling song, an aquatic rambling song, "Brandy" by Looking Glass. The main character sings about the woman who loves him, who works at a bar "layin' whiskey down." He says she's a fine girl and what a good wife she would be but, "my life, my love and my lady is the sea." How must that feel for poor Brandy? "I love you, babe. But you know what I love more? Being on a rickety tuna boat with a bunch of sweaty Portuguese guys."

The ads I really miss are the ones for cars and trucks. They used to be all about torque ratios, displacement, and fuel efficiency. Now they're about good vibes.

In 1976 I saw an ad for a Ford F-150. It showed the truck literally jumping over a sand dune while the voice-over bragged about its being "built Ford tough." The truck was featured in the Charles Bronson film *Mr. Majestyk*. Take a look. ( Q Google It ) **bit.ly/ ESA-Majestyk**

Compare that to truck ads today. In the past few years, I've seen two different ads for Toyota Tundras that made me want to ovulate. ( ⌕ Google It ) **bit.ly/ESA-Tundra1**

We see a group of people climb into a Toyota Tundra and drive out to an open field. They let down the tailgate to reveal spools of Christmas lights. We see them working into the night, wrapping them around trees and laying them out in the field. A light snow begins to fall as soft music plays. (I looked it up, and the song was by someone named Perfume Genius, which only adds to the faggotry.) Cut to lights from an aircraft in the distance, followed by the interior of the plane. A young female soldier (of course she's female, and of course, she's way better-looking than any actual young woman in the military) is looking out the window and sees that the lights spell out "Welcome Home, Julia." She sheds a single tear, as does her mother on the ground. The voice-over says, "Life is better when we celebrate together." Ugh. How does this make you want to buy a Tundra? How many people are in this situation? Show me a truck towing a boat. There's a much larger percentage of people who need the truck for that than touchy-feely "welcome home" messages. Also, how does this distinguish your brand? Are you somehow implying that Ram hates soldiers? Maybe it's overcompensation, since it seems like every time I see footage of ISIS with machine guns mounted on the back of pickup trucks, they're Toyotas. And, as my podcast announcer, Mike Dawson, points out, what if Julia was in the aisle seat?

Then there's this one, also for the Toyota Tundra. ( ⌕ Google It ) **bit.ly/ESA-Tundra2**

We see a family watching a *Friday Night Lights*–style high school football game from the stands. The quarterback throws a bomb to our protagonist, who catches it in the end zone. Touchdown! Inexplicably, the referee calls him out of bounds. The family, the kid, the team, and possibly the whole town are let down, as they've lost the playoff game. We see the family again, now driving home sadly in silence, in the rain, when they come upon a stranded motorist. He's got his car hood open and is getting drenched. The Tundra pulls up and, lo and behold, it's the ref who blew the call. The driver asks the ref if he needs a lift and tells his sons, both still in uniform, including the receiver who got jobbed, to make room. They share a look, and one of the sons slides over. With a nod, the father tells his son he's proud of him, and the son hands the ref a towel to dry off. As they pull away, up comes a graphic that says, "Let's Go Compassion."

Ugh. Let's go vomit. Are you selling trucks or tampons? It used to be about towing capacity and ground clearance. It was about how much shit you could pull or run over. Only now, in the era of the puss, would we try to sell trucks with compassion. Does compassion come standard, or is it an option? Do I get more compassion on the highway versus the city? What's the compassion capacity of this pickup?

## "Made with Love" Makes Me Hate

The worst commercials are the current run of Subaru ads featuring the slogan "Made with Love." What the fuck does that mean? Call me crazy, but I prefer my cars to be made with steel. Subaru is at the top of the leader board when it comes to pandering to pussies.

And, connected to my earlier rant on people and their support animals, there's a Subaru campaign featuring a family of dogs driving around the country with the tagline, "Dog Tested, Dog Approved." How fucked in the head are you if your line of thinking before an automotive purchase is, "I need to know that the thing currently dragging its asshole across my carpet would like this?"

Then there's the Subaru ad with the couple going hiking who stop in at a country store. They're young and hot, but you can't tell because he's dressed down and she's kinda frumped up and wearing a winter hat. She grabs a map and asks the old guy behind the counter if it shows "the peninsula trail." Another old guy sitting in the store, who looks like the bearded Oak Ridge Boy, ( 🔍 Google It ) **bit.ly/ESA-Oak** says, "You won't find that on a map," then stands up and reveals he's got a blind guy cane. After exchanging concerned looks, the couple decide to let him get in their Outback and guide them around to hear whales on the coast and owls in the woods. "Our Subaru Outback lets us see the world, sometimes in ways we never imagined." They're wandering around the woods in the pitch black with a crazed townie from the feed store. Because that's what happens in the real world. I'm pretty sure this is the beginning of an Eli Roth movie or a porn, because this couple is very adventurous. "Want to go wandering in the woods with a decrepit blind Santa Claus?" "Sure." I feel like you could easily talk this couple into swinging. By the way, just for some extra credit in the "woke" department, the Subaru ad people made the guy behind the counter black. You know, as most guys selling homemade granola outside of Portland are.

Last year I was at the Chicago Auto Show doing some promotion for Castrol. I'm a spokesman, and I was walking around looking at cars in between obligations. There was one area that had "The Jeep Experience," where you could drive over manmade hills. Guess what Subaru had? A dog adoption area complete with a "puppy kissing booth." Everyone else was talking about powertrain warranties, and Subaru was giving away Pomeranians. A big sign read, "Subaru Loves Pets." Nothing about horsepower. Plenty of puppy power but no horsepower. Again, they make a four-wheel-drive vehicle for all-terrain driving, but you wouldn't know it from any of their advertising. If you need something to drive to the ski resort, you might not know what to purchase, but if you're into "rescues," oh boy have they got a car for you.

When you purchase a Subaru, you receive a stash container with a big heart on it containing stickers of different feel-good activities you might be into, so you can put them on your bumper to let people know just how outdoorsy, earthy-crunchy, and back-packy you are. No joke. The stickers include, but are not limited to, scuba diving, food and wine, breast cancer awareness, kaya-king, antiquing, stargazing, and Ultimate Frisbee. They should have one for eating pussy, because the Outback is the biggest les-bian brand there is.

Methinks the brand doth protest too much. Subaru's aero-space division serves as a defense contractor for the Japanese government. In addition to making cars with love, they also make Apache helicopters with armor-piercing rounds. This is Ellen dancing at the beginning of every show. She doesn't want you to know she's a horrible person, so she does the hustle at the top of every taping. Subaru doesn't want you to know that they are also merchants of death, so they lean heavily on the lapdogs and leave out the attack helicopters.

Sadly, other brands with spotty histories have gotten in on the puppy party. Mercedes-Benz had an ad for their SUV where a young couple adopt a dog at a shelter and then take it out for ice cream. Mercedes, you made Hitler's six-wheeled car. Stop pre-tending you're the Mister Rogers of corporations.

## We'll Be Right Back After This Breaking of My Will to Live

When they're not trying to convince us with their touchy-feely ads that their corporation practices "compassionate capitalism" and their board of directors is "Up With People," ( Q Google It ) **bit.ly/ESA-Up** they're getting in on the everything-is-awful bandwagon and depressing the shit out of the masses. I was trying to watch football on a Sunday a few years back with the guys and Sonny when the NFL debuted its "No More" campaign. It was a silent sixty seconds with famous faces staring into the camera and holding back, and in some cases not holding back, tears as a statement against domestic violence. I don't want to sound like Maude Flanders, but how am I supposed to explain that to my kid? Seriously, Sonny is next to me at eight years old wondering why Antonio Gates is crying. Do I now need to explain to him how spousal abuse works, or do I concoct a lie that they're crying because the Chargers didn't cover the spread? That's why Daddy's crying. To top it off, it was immediately followed by a Cialis commercial, so I also had the opportunity to explain why the hotter-than-she-would-be-in-real-life wife looks sad that her silver fox husband's dick doesn't work.

It's especially jarring during the Super Bowl. That's supposed to be family time and definitely not supposed to be a bummer. I don't need to be inspired every second by people overcoming adversity. There was an ad in 2018; I can't even remember what it was for. I was a couple of IPAs in when I looked up at the TV and saw a woman born without legs, while soft Enya-style music was playing. How effective is your Super Bowl ad if I can't remember the product?

I do remember what they were advertising the year I looked up at the big screen during the big game to see an ad for a new medication to help with opioid-induced constipation. Not only do I have to think about people overdosing on Oxycontin, but now I also have to think about the fact that when they do eventually OD, they'll have fifty pounds of compacted shit in their colon like Elvis.

How fucking depressing is it that we have to watch an ad from a drug company for a medication to help with the dookie stoppage brought on by their other medication? And how fucking depressing is it to consider that this is such a big issue that they threw enough money at it to buy an ad during the Super Bowl? That's the Super Bowl of television-watching events.

Pharmaceutical ads are a bummer in general, and entirely unnecessary. They all end with "Talk to your doctor about Valzox" (a drug I made up but sounds real because, like the rest of them, it has a "v," a "z," and an "x" in it). If I have to talk to my doctor about it, why do you have to list the disgusting side effects I might experience? I'm at a bar watching the game with my butt on a stool; I don't want to think about blood *in* my stool. I need to take the antidepressant they're advertising because of the depression I got from their advertisement.

Again, it's all about trying to make us think that corporations care. Starbucks failed miserably with their #racetogether campaign in 2015, enlisting their baristas to start a dialogue about race with you as you awaited your venti no-foam macchiato. Starbucks doesn't give a fuck about solving the racial divide. The only black they care about is their yearly accounting being in the black. McDonald's had their "Pay With Lovin'" campaign, giving you forty-nine cents' worth of free grade-D burger if you hugged your dad in line or some shit. (Free food versus expressing affection would have been a real conundrum in the Carolla household of my youth.) McDonald's also had an ad with a children's choir singing "Carry On," showing signs outside their franchises with messages like "Remember 9/11," "Boston Strong," "Thank You Veterans," and "Pray for the Rescuers and Miners." Thank you, McDonald's, for that walk down tragedy lane. I had almost forgotten about 9/11. I appreciate the reminder. I was planning on erasing the worst day in American history from my memory, but your brave stance kept me on track. What the fuck? I'll assume you're pro-veteran and anti–Bin Laden. I don't need to know where Grimace stands on Al Qaeda.

The old McDonald's ads just listed the ingredients with a jingle. I bet you can still hear it in your head as you read this. "Two all-beef patties, special sauce, lettuce, cheese, pickles, onions on a sesame seed bun." That was good advertising. I'm fucking craving a Big Mac now. The point is, corporations used to just be corporations. Now they pretend to care about everyone because we're all needy douchebags. We don't need a personal relationship with our fast-food franchise. The food just has to taste good. That's it. It doesn't have to *feel* good. On that note, with all the class warfare stuff going on, I'm surprised we still have a Burger King. It's only a matter of time until the Bernie Sanders crowd tries to take him down for being a monarch and we end up with Burger Karl Marx.

Even internet porn got in on the depressing "awareness" bullshit. In 2015, Pornhub launched Pornhub Cares, offering a donation to a breast cancer charity each time you offered a donation to the crusty sock you keep under your bed while watching videos in the "Big Tits" and "Small Tits" categories.

> ( BTW ) Why is there even a "Small Tits" category? This must be because you can't have a "Fourteen-Year-Old Runaway" category. How low is your self-esteem if you're clicking on the "Small Tits" category? That's like watching a sports highlight reel called "Greatest Foul Balls." Not only is this an unnecessary downer—no one wants to think about breast cancer while staring at some double D's, except maybe in Germany—but they also missed an incredible opportunity. They should've called the campaign Spray It Forward. 😁

## People Who Don't Exist

When corporations and ad agencies are not mining tragedies and traumas to give you something to talk about in your next therapy session, they're painting unrealistic portraits either to create "I should have what that guy has" and "Look how that girl looks" envy or to fit the multicultural narrative being foisted on us every day. In my first book, I started complaining about the trend of making every burglar in home security ads a white guy, but in the decade since it's gone into Ludicrous Mode.

There is a Ring video doorbell ad with three robbers who are all white. In every other venture in commercials—having a garage band, a blind date, a political campaign, an office birthday party—there must be perfect racial balance. But if it's crime, it has to be whiter than an Osmond family reunion.

It got nuts with another Ring video doorbell commercial in which a melanin-free team of thieves steals packages from a doorstep. Not only is the main porch-pirate an attractive young white woman, but the victim is a black man. Here's where it gets absurd. As she's sneaking up, the Ring doorbell alerts his phone so he can see the unsavory character at his door. And he gets the call *while he's camping.* He's sitting around, alone, by a campfire. Has anyone ever seen a single black man camping solo? He's not part of some fake racially balanced Boy Scout excursion. Just a brother making s'mores all by his lonesome. The only way it could get faker is if he were fly fishing. I think it's time for us honkies to cry cultural appropriation

Then there's the LifeLock ad where all the hackers are white, which is fine. That's probably how it is in the real world—lots of Russians behind keyboards stealing your Social Security number—but I say turnabout is fair play. If all the home invaders in Ring doorbell ads have to have the skin pigment of Pete Buttigieg, then the hackers in LifeLock ads should have to look like T.I.

> **BTW** In all these ads where someone is stealing your identity via the internet, the perpetrators are always in some dank warehouse with their hoods up. Why do you need your sweatshirt hood over your head if you're committing the crime over the internet? It's not like someone's going to recognize you. 😶

There're plenty of people portrayed in ads who don't exist in the real world. There was an ad with a construction foreman with the aforementioned OIC, opioid-induced constipation. I worked construction with plenty of guys who were strung out on opioids, and none of them looked like that guy. He's wearing an untouched hard hat and clean boots and is carrying a thermos like he's from a Bugs Bunny cartoon. Clearly the person who handled wardrobe for the ad has never spent a minute on a construction site. When you're doing residential work, you don't wear a hard hat like you're one of the guys riveting girders while building a Vegas casino. It was literally a single-story home in the ad. There was nothing above the guy to fall on his hard-hatted head. Then, he's looking at blueprints on the hood of his not-beaten-to-shit pickup truck with a Hispanic guy and a black guy. Yep, a perfectly racially balanced construction crew, just like none that I was ever a part of. To complete the doesn't-actually-exist trifecta, the guy picks up his prescription from a good-looking white female doctor. Not sure where they all are in the real world. All the female doctors I've ever had were from somewhere bordering the Indian Ocean.

The only thing faker than this construction worker is the guy in a pest control commercial. There's a grand canyon between exterminators in commercials versus those who actually show up at your house. The guy in the ad looks like the third Hemsworth brother or a twenty-four-year-old Mike Rowe. He's got the belt tight, his shirt's clean, and his truck is spotless. He's firing a Hudson sprayer that's creating a force field to send bugs running. He's under the sink with a penlight plotting his next move and giving the homeowner all the details. He's got a cleft in his chin and a spring in his step. The guy who actually shows up in real life is a stubby Guatemalan who's haphazardly spraying your car or your cat while wearing a stained T-shirt with the front pocket falling off and asking to use your shitter.

Then there's the disparity between the woman shown in the bladder-control-medication ad versus who it would really be. On the screen she's a still-hot forty-four-year-old who dances before getting on the back of her man's motorcycle. On planet Earth, the middle-aged woman with a leakage problem isn't a hot chick dancing in a barn with her man and hopping on his Harley; she's a fat broad on a Lark scooter at Disneyland double-fisting churros.

Every commercial in which a guy meets a girl that involves mints or gum is incredibly fake. Both people are far too hot and could get laid without the Mentos breath. If a chick is hot enough, guys would fuck her even if she just ate a plate of used kitty litter. And it's not as if any good-looking chick would ever think, *Well, he looks like Danny DeVito, but his breath is an Arctic blast. I think I'll blow him.* These ads always take place in a far-too-clean and far-too-empty train or subway station. The people always pop the mint and kiss right before hopping onto some mass transit. I've never been in a train station that's empty. I've seen *The Warriors.* If your subway station is empty, run. No good-looking people choose this form of transportation; it's always homeless dudes who just shit themselves or guys playing saxophones for quarters. They're the ones who need Altoids, not the young Hollywood "It" couple.

The commercials that drive me the most nuts are for Peloton. These feature the hottest chick in the world, who apparently lives in an empty modern art museum and rocks it on a stationary bike at six a.m. She's twenty-six but has two kids who look like they're nine, and she's making them waffles after doing a power hour on her bike at the Guggenheim, all before the sun comes up. The real version is this: her husband gets up at 7:45 a.m. to start getting ready for work, turns on the bathroom light, and she moans from the bed, "What are you doing?!"

> BTW These Peloton bikes are a real "Fuck you" to the nations where riding a bicycle is the only non-animal form of transportation. "Yeah, we have bikes, but they don't go anywhere, and we ride them for exercise because we don't burn any calories digging wells."

I see this nonexistent wife in mattress commercials, too. There's one that stands out in which the wife has short dark hair and piercing blue eyes, and is happy to go to bed. She's wearing a very comfortable-looking silk nightie that no real woman has ever slept in. There's nothing on the nightstand—no moisturizers, magazines, or earplugs. In the non-fantasy version of this, she's wearing Cookie Monster pajama bottoms and a decade-old Aerosmith concert T-shirt, and the nightstand is covered in a dog-eared *US Weekly* and a pump-squirt bottle of hand lotion. Plus the drawer is buzzing because she accidentally turned on her vibrator while reaching into the nightstand to retrieve her anti-teeth-grinding nightguard.

The Christmas Peloton commercial made me particularly Grinchy. There is a little bit of irony, as I first saw this commercial while sitting on the couch with Lynette eating a bowl of pasta and watching TMZ. The premise is that a husband has bought his already skinny, smoking-hot wife a Peloton for Christmas, and has stored it out in the woodshed behind the house until the holiday arrives. The siren song of the stationary bike is so strong that even though it's a gift for her, he can't resist using it himself.

The first thing that pissed me off was the clock. This unreal dude pops up at 5:03 a.m. without the aid of an alarm. (An alarm would wake up his sleeping beauty of a wife.) He just gets up because he's so fucking pumped to hop on the Peloton. He runs out to the shed, uncovers it—because he has hidden it under a big blanket, as if the wife couldn't determine what it was due to the poncho he's tossed over it—and rides. They show him do this several more times. He runs out in a snowstorm—it's Christmastime, after all—does a couple hot laps on the Peloton, then jumps back into bed hoping to go unnoticed. Except for the fact that he's sweating. Doesn't he think that's going to raise suspicion? "Why are you all sweaty?" "Um…got up to make coffee. We were all out, so I walked to Starbucks, and then I got chased by a Kodiak bear. Killed it with a scone."

You don't want to know the real-life version of this guy. He's got body dysmorphic disorder.

I don't like anyone who works out before the sun comes up, unless they're high on coke.

You don't need to buy your wife a gift seven months in advance. You can have it delivered two days before Christmas. You certainly don't need the name tag that says "Jill" on it. It seems to just be the two of them; I don't think the gift needs to be labeled. And women in general aren't fond of getting exercise equipment as gifts. If the chick in this commercial wasn't already a ten, she'd be crying on Christmas morning.

> ( BTW ) I'd make a terrible Peloton trainer. They're supposed to be inspirational and motivational and can't be cruel. I would be the R. Lee Ermey of Peloton trainers. I wouldn't even be on a bike. I'd be in a La-Z-Boy chain-smoking, eating key lime pie, and shouting, "If this stationary bike was hooked up to a generator connected to the dome light of a '73 Impala, it'd be dim, you bloated witch. I don't care how hard you pedal, cunt, you'll never outrun your horrible childhood." I should create a side hustle for myself around my particular gift for shaming. I'd call it "I Have No Soul Cycle."

There was one ad that hit the jackpot as far as pissing me off. Like the Peloton ads, it features a wife who's too pretty for reality pedaling her ass off on a stationary bike, but this one also uses the well-worn, untrue trope of the lazy buffoon of a dad who doesn't deserve his hardworking hero of a wife. It's for Applebee's. To the tune of Dion's "Runaround Sue," Mom gets up at six a.m., walks the dog, takes a spin class, heads to the ER—yep, she's a doctor—then hugs a large woman of color in the hospital. By the time she leaves, it's dark out, but she has to stop and pick up the dry cleaning. Then she gets a text from her husband that reads, "Thoughts on dinner?" She hops on her phone, orders some Applebee's for curbside pickup, grabs it, and walks into her house to find her husband having a "Floss" dance party with the kids. And then comes the peak fakeness: She has a warm "Oh, you guys" smile on her face. We then see her eating a salad while he chomps down on a burger. Bullshit. This wife would be beleaguered. She'd throw the burger at him and collapse in a heap of tears, and the next item on her to-do list would be to call a divorce lawyer. Imagine if you switched sexes in this ad. There would be outrage. You'll never see something coming out of Madison Avenue where a male doctor walks the dog, hits the gym, attends to the kids on the burn unit, picks up the dry cleaning and dinner, and comes home to find his wife goofing around with the kids.

## If There's Toxic Masculinity, Then I'm the Toxic Avenger

My outrage at Madison Avenue peaked during the Super Bowl in 2019 when Gillette debuted their "Is This the Best a Man Can Be?" ad taking down so-called toxic masculinity. Men have always been idiots in ads, pouring waffle batter into the toaster and fucking up building a doghouse, but now we're not just being portrayed as dolts, we're being portrayed as evil.

The only guy in TV ads who's not a total moron, monster, or puss is the dude from the Ultimate Flashlight commercials. He starts off by saying, "Former Green Beret colonel Duke Lacrosse here." He's standing on top of a boulder with an eagle circling his head, explaining that his military-grade titanium tactical light is going to make your current flashlight its bitch. He then sets out to destroy his flashlight by freezing it in a block of ice, running it over with a Humvee, and burning it overnight in a campfire. It's all very impressive, and as I'm reaching for my credit card I have this thought, *If your flashlight survives an overnight fire, that means you got drunk and fell asleep with a lit cigarette during a power outage. If your flashlight is frozen in a block of ice, the good news is that it still works and could be presented to your son as a reminder that eighty-six Americans die every year ice fishing. And if your flashlight gets run over by a truck, the last thing you were doing with it was feverishly signaling the guy behind the wheel of the big rig shouting, "Take out your earbuds!"*

( BTW ) I love these "As Seen on TV" products. I knew they were going to phase out the penny, but I didn't realize they'd already taken a ton out of circulation and infused all that copper into socks, underwear, shirts, and work gloves. The ads always have some aged NFL player saying, "I can use my hands again, thanks to my Copper Fit gloves," or "My knees don't ache, thanks to my copper-infused leggings," or "My wife had five orgasms last night, thanks to my Copper Fit condom." Gotta admit, I'm a sucker for this stuff. I'm covered in more copper right now than the Statue of Liberty. 😁

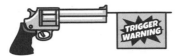

If you're one of the people who likes the Gillette ad about toxic masculinity, you're not gonna like the next few pages. Razor ads have always pissed me off. They all feature twenty-four-year-old guys with clean, well-lit, amazing bathrooms. They all live in the W Hotel. And then a hot chick sidles up to feel his baby-bottom-smooth face. When I was twenty-four, I had nine roommates in my bathroom. One was usually passed out in the tub covered in his own vomit, and another would put my toothbrush up his butt as a prank.

( Q Google It ) **bit.ly/ESA-Gillette** Opening on a montage of men looking at themselves in mirrors with audio of fake Me Too, bullying, and "toxic masculinity" news clips playing underneath, the ad then has a somber voice-over of someone asking, "Is this the best a man can get?" Then a boy is being chased by a group of older kids while text messages pop up on the screen saying, "You're such a loser," "Sissy," and "Everyone hates you!" Of course, the bullies are white. Perfect racial balance in the part of the ad where guys do the right thing, but the villains certainly can't have ancestors from anywhere other than Europe. In the second half of the ad, there are two vignettes where black men stop white guys from acting inappropriately. I've heard of being my brother's keeper, but it seems from this ad that the brothers are keeping us.

The voice-over says, "We can't hide from it. It's been going on far too long," as we see shots of wolf-whistle cartoons from the '40s, a fake sitcom from the '60s with a guy grabbing a maid's ass, and a fake rap video with chicks dancing in bikinis. But the part that pisses me off the most is the moment when two boys are wrestling in a backyard and dads in a long line at charcoal grills with hot dogs and ears of corn say repeatedly in unison, "Boys will be boys."

Yes, boys *will* be boys. Because boys *are* boys. Stop thinking you can change that and make them girls. One guy steps away from the grill, breaks up the scuffle, and says, "This is not how we treat each other." Yes it is, Mrs. Mister. It's two five-year-olds roughhousing on the lawn at a barbecue. It's what they do. I sure hope we don't get into another war or need to build a bridge or a skyscraper, because we'd be fucked. The Russians and Chinese must love how big a pile of pussies we're becoming. They've got to be preparing an invasion. The boys weren't throwing punches; neither busted out brass knuckles or started curb-stomping the other. Guys scrap with other guys. This is a fucking fact of nature. It's instinct. Every male mammal on the planet goes through a period of rough-and-tumble play to learn where the boundaries are and how to be assertive without being aggressive, how to defend itself, and how to bond with other creatures in its colony, tribe, pod, whatever. It's called horsing around because it's something that horses do. This is anthropology. Stop trying to wish it away with good vibes.

I've regaled readers of my memoir, *Not Taco Bell Material*, with many stories of being punched, kicked, spit on, pissed on, shit on, embarrassed, and generally bullied by my best friends growing up. It's part of the process. My fans know my friend Ray well. In case you are new to the Carolla-verse, there's a whole chapter on him in that book. We played football together, so there were a lot of locker room shenanigans, usually involving urine. Here's one I didn't include in that book that Gillette and our new society would find highly problematic. Ray would get a running start and whip a full bar of soap at you in the group shower while you were naked. If that hit you in the eye or the dick, you'd be going to the ER. It would be like Wayne Gretzky taking a slap shot at your noggin. Guys would be hiding behind other guys trying not to get concussed by Irish Spring. Then there was the time he broke off the top of a shampoo bottle and tried to jam the jagged opening into our openings, if you catch my meaning. Thankfully the coach came in and put a stop to the Pert Plus anal-rape experience.

Now that's bullying. What is depicted in this ad isn't. In high school, my buddy Tom, the black son of a hand surgeon, had a big house in the hills with a diving board. (How's that for breaking stereotypes? Big house, hand surgeon, swimming—not the top three things that come to mind when talking about the brothers.) The diving board extended a good six feet over the end of the pool. At night, me, Tom, and the other guys we hung out with would go to Tom's house, get naked, and take turns at the end of the diving board while the next nude dude in line would come up, and we'd grapple. You'd throw him into the pool, or he'd toss you in. You got to stay up there as long as you could. That was Saturday night. It was naked teenage *American Gladiators*. This was perfectly normal behavior for us.

The Gillette ad might just as well have featured guys shaving their legs, tucking their junk between their legs, and trimming a nice vaginal landing-strip pube patch, because apparently the best a man can get is to become a woman. It ends with the voice-over saying, "The boys watching today will be the men of tomorrow." No they won't, because there won't be any men. The dudes I know who are pussies are doing far more damage to society than any of the "toxic" males I know. As I've said before, any wounds you get from a fight are temporary. Being a pussy is a lifetime sentence. We wouldn't have Navy SEALs if the guys instructing them didn't bully them. Bin Laden would still be alive today if someone hadn't told Navy SEAL Rob O'Neill he was worthless and weak and needed to do another hundred push-ups.

Not being compassionate, not being kind, and not being honest are bad things that we should correct, but we don't need to run from being tough. Tough is a good thing in a society where people do try to take advantage of you, where you do have hardships. It's right there in the word. To get through hard*ship* you need some hard*ness*. Why the same group preaching all the victimhood stuff I talked about earlier is so invested in also getting everyone to be so soft is beyond me. How can you simultaneously tell people that everyone is out to get them but that they should also get soft? You should be soft when it comes to some elements of how you raise your kids, but you should also be hard when it comes to discipline or protecting your family. Both things can be true. We need nuance. We need to be able to live in a world where we can go soft and get hard as needed. Sorry if I got a little phallic at the end there.

# Chapter 5

# Hashtag Heroes

W e live in the era of social media. I don't consider myself an "influencer," but I am drunk right now, so I'll consider myself an under-the-influencer. I have never personally used Facebook, but I am active on Twitter. I have a blue check mark next to my name, which means I'm official, that it's not someone pretending to be me. As if anyone else could come up with the pearls and nuggets I dispense on a daily basis, such as, "Get it on," "true," and "me and drew call now." I don't have "the real" in front of my Twitter handle, though I do think it would be a power move for someone who cleans pools or drives a bakery truck to put "the real" in front of their name to make it seem like they have some juice.

I'm not even sure what my Twitter profile says under my name, but apparently, it's gauche to brag because I saw that Obama's profile says, "Dad, husband, President, citizen." If I were him, it would say, "President, President, President, knows Jay-Z, President." It's all part of our shitty, envy-filled culture in which successful people have to pretend to not be successful. Fuck that.

To whichever of the social media monkeys I employ who works my Twitter feed, please change my bio to "Literally a Millionaire, 3x *New York Times Bestseller*, 2x Guinness World Record Holder: Most Downloaded Podcast and World's Girthiest Penis."

Of course you're going to put yourself in the best light or humblebrag. The new rule is that your ex should have to write your Twitter bio so we can get to the truth. I'd love to see the more honest Twitter bios that result from that. Some poor gal would have a bio that reads, "Bitch Is Always Late. Can't Cook for Shit. Stinky Snatch." And some unlucky dude's would say, "Unemployable. Deadbeat Dad. Cries While Beating Off."

## Casualties of Twitter "Wars"

I have never been in a so-called Twitter war. I find that term offensive. You know who else would be offended? Guys who fought in actual wars. I'd like to go to Normandy and resurrect everyone who was gunned down on the beaches, show them an argument between Donald Trump and Chrissy Teigen, and say, "This is what a war is now."

I'm sad to say that even my man-wife, Jimmy Kimmel, got wrapped up in one. After making a joke on his show about Melania Trump—by the way, he's a monster; I'd never do anything like that, especially in this book three chapters ago—Sean Hannity took to Twitter calling Jimmy "Harvey Weinstein Jr." among other insults. Jimmy shot back. It escalated, and Jimmy eventually wrote, "When your clown makeup rubs off on Trump's ass, does it make his butt look like a Creamsicle?" before stepping away and moving on with his life. I have a simple policy. If the combined age of the two people feuding is over one hundred, they should just move on.

People try to incite these "wars," like when two kids are arguing on the bus or the playground and everyone stands around them chanting, "Fight, fight, fight!" At some point I made a negative comment on my podcast regarding David Letterman, along the lines of not wanting to work for him. I know some people who have worked for him, and the general impression I got was that he was difficult to say the least, a dick to say the most. Well, some pussy had to tweet to Jimmy and say, "Did you hear what Adam had to say about your idol?" I'm sure Jimmy hadn't and would have lived his life just fine without that information. More important, he's too fucking busy to listen to the podcast and get the context, so he's forced to assume I was saying shit about the man he regards as his mentor. This is the chick gossip-queen gene run amok. A decade ago, when I wrote *In Fifty Years We'll All Be Chicks*, this behavior was reserved mostly for women and some dudes I'd never want to hang out with. But social media has weaponized the tattletale "I just thought you should know" assholes I complained about at the time. These guys gain nothing from this behavior. It's not like Twitter is a program where you get $1.95 every time you rat out a celebrity for talking shit.

I've found that the best move when someone is critical of me on Twitter is to kill them with kindness. To be clear, I'm not contradicting my earlier declaration about not apologizing, but I'm willing to own my mistakes or acknowledge a genuine grievance. No one likes it when they read a tweet that takes them to task. But you shouldn't reflexively tweet back, "Eat a Dick!" Take it in for a second and see if the person has a point. Find out what they disagree with, be a man, own it, and move on if it's true. Here's a good personal example.

You might know the name Terri Schiavo, but here's a quick recap in case you don't. She was at the center of a big right-to-die legal case in Florida in the '90s. In 1990 she suffered a heart attack and was resuscitated but had severe brain damage. She was only twenty-six years old, which is insane statistically. This left her in a vegetative state. A legal feud between her husband and parents ensued, with him arguing that she would not have wanted to live that way and them fighting to keep her on the feeding tube, which was removed and reinserted several times based on the latest court ruling in the case. Jeb Bush, governor of Florida at the time, passed "Terri's Law" to protect her and keep her on the feeding tube. This became a national issue, with civil libertarians and the religious right taking their respective sides. In March 2005, the tube was finally removed and Terri died shortly after.

( BTW ) For the record, as an atheist, I think it's selfish to keep people in that state on life support. I blame Hollywood for making too many *Awakenings*-type movies with guys coming out of comas. It would be funny, though, to see someone wake up in 2020 from a coma that started in 2000. "The World Trade Center was taken out in a terrorist attack, we're in two wars, every kid has their own TV station on a website called YouTube, we all take pictures of every meal we eat, Prince and Michael Jackson are dead, Bill Cosby is in prison for rape, and Donald Trump is president." The guy would pull his own plug. 😬

As far as Terri Schiavo is concerned, in *President Me* I wrote:

*Before I move on from vegetables to other areas covered by the USDA, I ought to name a Secretary of Agriculture. I'm going with Terry Schiavo. Not just because she was the world's most famous vegetable but because she's no longer with us and I'm committed to reducing the size of government.*

In 2019 I received a tweet from her brother, Bobby Schindler, which reads:

*It recently came to my attention what you wrote about my deceased sister, Terri Schiavo, in your book,* President Me. *Perhaps the next time you decide to target an innocent disabled woman with your crude humor, you will spell her name correctly.*

First off, the typo is something my cowriter, editor, copy editor, and proofreader should have caught, but it was my joke, and I owned it. I replied simply, "Sorry if I caused you any pain." (Actually, looking back on the Twitter timeline, I see that I wrote, "Sorry if a caused you any pain." As I mentioned, I'm not great at working the Twitter machine. ( Q Google It ) **bit.ly/ESA-Schindler**

The point is that he was taken aback by my sincere apology. He replied, "That wasn't the response I was expecting. So thank you, I appreciate it."

Twitter is not as uncivilized as we make it out to be. You would think that 50 percent of the time the person who critiqued you would come back with "fuck you anyway." More often than not, however, they accept it, which reminds me of another story about a guy named Carter Lay. If the last name sounds familiar, it's because he was the heir to the thirteen-billion-dollar Frito-Lay empire. I met him doing the Long Beach celebrity Grand Prix in 2014. Not only was he rich, but he had beaten leukemia and started a charity around it.

On the day of the race, we were hanging out, and I was noticing his custom helmet and expensive racing shoes. When you do these celebrity pro-am races, everyone is issued standard shoes by a company called Simpson that are worth about thirty-four dollars. But if your family basically invented stoner chow, you can afford three-hundred-dollar custom kicks. He had Pumas with a titanium insert, and when I asked why they laced up on the side, he told me that laces on the top could cut off circulation in your foot. High-tech stuff. There was more technology in this guy's shoes than there was in the Carolla household my entire childhood.

Unfortunately, he was one of the slower guys, and I lapped him five minutes into the race.

On my all-things-automotive podcast, CarCast, I proceeded to make fun of him. This billionaire had top-of-the-line shoes, the same that F1 drivers wear, and they didn't help one iota. It would be as if a guy showed up to the Pebble Beach pro-am with his own custom carbon-fiber golf club, teed up, swung, and immediately hooked the ball into the Pacific.

Another "Just thought you should know" dickhead thought the billionaire philanthropist cancer survivor should just know that the C-list podcaster was talking shit about him and his expensive shoes. That day Carter sent me a tweet, and I was thinking, *Fuck. There's no way he heard the clip, so he probably thinks I was being a real asshole instead of just busting chops.*

He tweeted me: "I was going to respond to @adamcarolla remarks on the radio today but I'm just glad I left a lasting impression #RealStoryLater."

I thought about how I could shoot back with, "Hey, billionaire, why don't you thicken up that skin," or, "Fuck you, I have a pirate ship, I can say whatever I want," or "You're too uptight—maybe you need to get Layd."

Instead, I simply replied with: "@CarterLay sorry for that, I didnt mean to sound so douche."

You could tell that was my genuine tweet due to my genuine typos in "didn't" (fuck apostrophes) and "douchey" (the real douche is autocorrect, which changes it to "douche" when you type that).

Well, he simply tweeted back: "@adamcarolla Hahahha you're the best loved meeting you."

It didn't need to be a "war."

The reason this story is different than the Terri Schiavo one is that a few months after that back-and-forth, I found out he died at the relatively young age of forty-four. I was relieved I hadn't been a dick and that our last exchange hadn't been negative. Tweets are short. You know what else is? Life. Don't waste time entrenching yourself when you've said something impulsive and insultive (I know that's not a word, but it flowed).

People often get hyperbolic and say that certain tweets, typically those of Donald Trump and other right-leaning folk, are inciting violence and that those doing the tweeting should be banned from the platform. This is bullshit. The same type of people who now claim Trump is inciting violence with tweets are also those who formerly argued against the idea that music and video games incite violence. If Marilyn Manson's and N.W.A.'s lyrics or *Grand Theft Auto* and *Red Dead Redemption* aren't causing mass shootings, then neither are Trump's tweets. You have to be logically consistent, not logically convenient.

In general, my Twitter rule is this: If you wouldn't say it in an elevator, you shouldn't tweet it. It should take the same effort to talk shit online as it used to take before social media existed. Before you send out that ill-informed tweet calling me a bigot because I had Dinesh D'Souza on my show, you should have to walk to your nearest post office, drop fifty-five cents (the current price of a stamp as I write this) into the trash can, and walk back before you hit Send. You should have to go through the same process as sending someone a letter. By the time you walk back from the post office, you'll probably have cooled off. I had a bit that I never got on *The Man Show* about a phone breathalyzer for drunk dialers. We need to put something in place for all the assholes with no impulse control who are so eager to hit the Tweet button.

## You're Not Offended, and Fuck You if You Are

Sadly, people don't use social media for its true intended purpose—retweeting funny shit that I say on my podcast, which is basically all I use it for. Twitter used to be a place to crack 140-character jokes, let people know about your yard sale, and share a video of your cat falling into the pool. Somewhere along the way, and definitely after Trump got into the race in 2016, it became an out-rage factory trying to keep up with the holiday rush. It's not that there's more stuff to be outraged about; it's that people are get-ting outraged *for* other people. When did we become empowered to defend people we've never met and have no connection with? Especially around race. Any perceived racial slight, even as a joke, is treated like Pearl Harbor.

There has never been a better time to actually be a racist, because you get lumped in with me and other comedians. Let me give you a couple of personal anecdotes related to white people overcompensating and being outraged on behalf of black people who couldn't give a fuck about me and my jokes.

I was at the Monterey Historics, a weekend event full of vintage cars, featuring the Concours d'Elegance, a viewing overlooking the Pacific Ocean with cars on display that are worth more than the GDP of several African nations combined. The guys there are dripping in wealth. They wear four-thousand-dollar blazers with T-shirts underneath, ascots, and loafers that cost more than the bed or couch you're reading this on. These are the kind of guys who count their money in bundles.

Me and my crew were at a table with another rich honky. He was going on about his 1950s Zagato bodied Maserati blah blah blah that they only made eleven of, while well-dressed waiters and waitresses topped off our champagne. I chimed in after he talked about how it was made in Turin and how it felt to drive it on the Amalfi Coast. I said, "You know this is what black people think white people do all day."

There was an educated middle-aged white woman with him who took great umbrage at my joke. This wasn't the ditzy arm candy of some rich dude. Before the joke even landed, she said "Whoa, don't go there." I replied, "No, I'm making a joke about us." She continued to protest, "All right, Mr. Comedian…" She heard the word "black" and just assumed it was offensive. She was so racially sensitive and suffering from secondhand outrage, she had to protest.

Then, recently, I was at the Ice House, a comedy club in Pasadena, doing a little vignette involving race. I said, "I did my family history on Ancestry.com. And it's a tricky thing nowadays. They're finding out stuff about people's pasts and their families. Even if it's a distant relative, they're holding it against you now. It could hurt your career. I don't know who my great-great grandpappy was and what he might have done. So I was a little nervous. I got the results back yesterday, and it's worse than I could imagine. It said *current* slave owner."

A black chick in the back of the room laughed and said out loud, "No, you didn't!" She got it. The joke was about my being a racist. As I went on to the next bit, a woman not of color, your standard-issue twenty-seven-year-old L.A. white chick, chimed in. I said, "Look, I'm trying to heal the racial divide. Black folks know how to play the game of dominoes. White people set dominoes up on their edge, knock them over, and laugh maniacally. 'Look, it's my initials!' We don't know how to play dominoes. If the black community could reach out to their white brothers and teach us how to actually play the game of dominoes, I think there could be a lot of healing. It's a two-way street. I would do the same. If I saw a group of black guys with a chessboard and they were just knocking the pieces over and laughing like lunatics, I'd intervene."

This white chick, her arms folded, tsk-tsked me. "Oh no. NN-nnn." So I started arguing with her. "Okay, so everyone knows how to play the game of dominoes evenly?" Nothing. "No? Okay, white people know how to play the game of dominoes *more* than black people?" She grunted disapprovingly. "Okay, some white people know how to play dominoes and some black people know how to play dominoes." She was okay with that. Until I altered the joke so there was no difference between the two groups, until there was nothing to contrast, she expressed her discontent. Which is exactly how not to do comedy.

My point is this: Did those "marginalized" people ask for your protection? No? Then why are you treating them like children who can't fend for themselves? If you truly care about "marginalized" people, you'll afford them the dignity to defend themselves against the outrageous hurtful comments of guys doing late-night sets at small comedy clubs in Pasadena. If you *are* in that group, you can be offended. You shouldn't be, but you can be. But if you're not a member of the group being mocked, you can't be an offense agent taking 15 percent of the outrage.

## Cultural Appropriation Is the Sincerest Form of Flattery

Fake outrage gets particularly nutty when we get into the area of "cultural appropriation." We're not talking about Al Jolson black-face; we're talking about white women opening up a burrito stand and guys dressing up as mariachis at parties. Both of these are true stories. Two women in Portland had their burrito business shut down because of "cultural appropriation" protests after they bragged about going to Mexico and peeking into kitchen windows to learn how to make authentic tortillas, and the president of the University of Louisville was forced to apologize for wearing a poncho, sombrero, and bushy mustache and holding maracas for a Mexican-themed Halloween costume.

It's such bullshit. Anyone who actually wears a sombrero couldn't possibly be offended by this. The purpose of a sombrero and its super-wide rim is to keep the sun off you while you toil in Mexican deserts. If you need that hat, and thus have the right to be offended by someone wearing it ironically, then you have too much other shit going on to be offended. You're not worried about a frat boy wearing your native headwear on Cinco de Mayo; you're worried about well water.

It's not just hysteria on behalf of Hispanics. There were fake outrage and online protests about Disney's *Moana* Halloween costumes. Disney has attempted to do the right thing by diversifying and having princesses of color. Go back and look at how the Indians were portrayed in *Peter Pan*. They were savages. Or dig deep and look at *Song of the South*, which is not surprisingly hard to find on store shelves. Disney and all of Hollywood could tell which way the wind was blowing at the turn of century, so they started checking all the racial boxes. Mulan, Asian. Check.

99

Pocahontas, Native American. Check. Jasmine, Middle Eastern. Check. Tiana, black. Check. Then came Moana. During the run-up to Halloween, Disney tried to make a couple of bucks merchandising their latest nonwhite Snow White, and some Caucasian douche had to get his or her panties in a bunch about it. Do you know who suffered? The little Hawaiian, Samoan, and Polynesian girls who finally had a princess who looked like them.

It's a fucking Halloween costume. No harm is going to be done. Nor is any good. This does not affect anyone's life in any way. I'd like to say to whoever rang the alarm bells and got to feel like a hero for rescuing a damsel who wasn't in distress, next time give the story a real fairy-tale ending—put a trash bag over your head, give yourself a duct tape dickey, and let us all live happily ever after.

( BTW ) I've long complained about Olympic fencing, and I have a fix that involves some cultural garb, but first a jag on the sport itself. I realized during the 2012 Olympics, when all we could talk about was swimming and Michael Phelps, that fencing was done. It's sword fighting. It should have been the most exciting event, but all we were talking about was swimming.

One problem is that it's over before it begins. The fencers stand eight feet apart, someone hits an airhorn and, by the time you blink, they're taking their masks off. You don't even know who won or why. No one ever gets cut, then tastes their own blood and announces, "Now I shall avenge the death of my father!"

I can fix this. First, you know how there's a compulsory part in skating, when the skaters have to pull off certain moves? We should do the same with fencing. To start, the fencers would

100

have to slice all the candles off a candelabra, followed by the part in which they flip their opponent's sword to him with their foot after he drops it. Then they would close by putting a "Z" in the opponent's shirt without cutting him, and slashing a rope to drop a chandelier that traps eight henchmen.

Here's my second solution, which I am genuinely in love with. This is not a joke. We should make the Olympian fencers wear the garb and use the weapons associated with their nation's history. How high would the ratings be if instead of two guys in beekeeper costumes, it was a contender from Japan in a Samurai kimono with a katana going up against a Norwegian athlete wearing a Viking helmet and a fur vest and wielding a battle axe? A French Olympian would be dressed as the fourth Musketeer with a thin, pointed blade, while a Saudi competitor would be holding a giant scimitar and wearing the outfit of the guy who got shot by Indiana Jones in *Raiders of the Lost Ark*.

I know this could work. It would have to, because right now Olympic fencing is less interesting to watch than Mexican day laborers putting up actual fencing. 😁

It used to be the church folk who cared about this stuff, the uptight religious-right folks who started petitions to have "satanic" costumes removed, the Tipper Gores of the world. Now, it's the exact opposite. It's the people who are supposed to be the "Let your freak flag fly" crowd who are suppressing everything. They need to take their own advice and move on dot org.

It gets particularly stupid when it comes to mascots, team names, and logos. The Washington Redskins controversy finally died down after a *Washington Post* survey showed that nine out of ten Native Americans were not offended. Ten out of ten douchebags on Twitter and in the comments section of HuffPost were offended for them, so they didn't need to be offended. I don't think redskins are big fans of the pigskin—Native Americans are not huge football watchers. That didn't stop Cal State, Long Beach, from getting rid of their Prospector Pete mascot, which became the target of Golden State social justice warriors because the Gold Rush led to the killing of indigenous people. And in 2015, Governor Jerry Brown signed a law banning public schools in the state from adopting the Redskins moniker for their teams. At the time it was passed, there were only four schools using the name and they were given two years to get rid of it. Good job, Jerry. Way to work small to big. Can we please focus on traffic now? Let's worry less about the redskins and more about the red lights.

The real problem with the focus on these nonsense issues is satiation. It just stops you from actually doing anything that will have a genuine effect. As if stopping a school from using a mascot is actually going to accomplish anything for the community you do-gooders are trying to protect. It's like feeding hungry children a boot full of sawdust. They'd announce they're full, and you'd announce your work is done. As if we could just get rid of Uncle Ben and Aunt Jemima, and the black community would have the ship turned around in no time. Think about the actual problems that plague the Native American community and imagine explaining to their faces that you've been working really hard on the mascot problem. "Hey, tutors who were heading to the reservation, turn around, problem solved. Cancel the orders for insulin and substance abuse counselors. Prospector Pete is gone."

The only upshot of this stupidity is that it led to one of my favorite bits from an animated pilot I did for Fox in 2012. My character, Mr. Birchum, was the woodshop teacher at George

Washington Junior High School, but the PC crowd did their thing with the school's name, sign, and mascot. ( ⌕ Google It ) **bit.ly/ ESA-Birchum**

## The Cult of Correction

The word wardens' efforts are not about a love of black and brown people. They're about a love of correcting, especially correcting old white guys.

Let's do a little quiz. See if you can pick the correct pronunciation for the following words.

Carnegie:
   a. Car-NAYgee
   b. CAR-neh-gee
Cannes:
   a. Can
   b. Cahn
Iraq:
   a. Eee-ROCK
   b. Eye-RACK
Qatar:
   a. Cuh-TAR
   b. Cutter

The correct answer is...

It doesn't fucking matter how you pronounce them, the Huff-Post crowd will correct you. As soon as you figure out how to say something the way they want, they'll change it so they can have dominion over you. That's what they do. They change accents and syllables, even pronouns, just to give themselves the power to correct you.

I find this whole pronunciation problem very di-VISS-ive. Or do I mean di-VI-sive?

We're constantly changing the terms. With all the PC stuff on planes, such as removing the words "cockpit" and "stewardess," it's only a matter of time before we also get rid of "class." How dare we use terms that imply one group is better than the other, even though that other group paid more money and gets perks for it? I heard recently that "Eskimo" is no longer an appropriate term. Why? Was "Eskimo" offensive in some way? Can we still call an Eskimo pie an Eskimo pie? Just because whitey labeled you with it eighty years ago doesn't make it derogatory. For a very "woke" group, I'm surprised they're still using the term *boy*cott. Shouldn't it be *cis*cott by now?

I could do an entire chapter on the "preferred pronoun" bullshit and the gender-versus-sex stuff. Those definitions change more often and with more drama than the drag queens employing those monikers. The correct terms around gender and sex are as stable in today's society as a fucking lava lamp. The city of Berkeley, California, became a parody of itself last year when it banned all gender-specific words in city ordinances and documents. The word "manhole" was replaced with "maintenance hole," "manpower" was out and "human effort" was in, and even "pregnant woman" was ousted for "pregnant employee." "Fraternity" and "sorority" were replaced with "collegiate Greek system resident," and "craftsman" was replaced by "artisan." Congratulations, you replaced the word "manhole," but you're still an "asshole."

The San Francisco area is the tip of the spear (a term that I'm sure someone will find offensive) when it comes to this change-the-language-to-feel-good bullshit. The San Francisco Board of Supervisors recently changed the language they use in meetings and documents so that "convicted felons" are now referred to as "justice-involved persons," "parolees" are now "returning residents," and an "addict" is now referred to as "a person with a history of substance abuse." So, on your next trip to San Fran, you can look forward to "a person with a history of substance abuse" who is "a returning resident" after being "justice-involved" "relieving" you of your wallet at an ATM while a "helping friendly patrol person," formerly known as a "police officer," is busy with the used-to-be "homeless" now "non-housed person" who was a babbling "schizophrenic" but now is known as a "non-reality-bound citizen."

Just to be balanced, there is a right-leaning version of this too—gun guys. Unlike masturbators, they are not quiet about their hobby. They want everyone to know they love guns, and that includes correcting you on your firearm faux pas. To all my NRA-member fans reading this, I don't know, nor do I give a fuck, about the difference between a clip and a magazine.

This whole language correction thing is retarded. Yes, I use that word very fucking intentionally. As a car guy, I am offended by the attack on the word "retarded." In a car, you either advance or retard the engine timing. It simply means to slow something down. Being mentally retarded means your mental growth was slowed down. As if calling someone "developmentally delayed" makes a fucking difference in the misery that condition causes to that person and their family. I got some pushback from a previous publisher about using that term, but I did not let her retard me in my use of the word "retard." That would make me retarded. Out of curiosity, I did a word search and found that the "retard" count from my previous books is fifty-two. So, with this paragraph, I just got up to an even sixty.

## Social Media—a Virtual Soapbox for Virtue-Signaling

In America, we think we can make problems vanish with slogans. Drug problem? "Just Say No." Car fatalities? "Click It or Ticket." Dropouts? "No Child Left Behind." Done. That's the bullshit that politicians employ to make it seem like they care. Now, it has become the pastime of the civilian as well in the form of hashtags. Twitter, Facebook, and Instagram are littered with people standing on digital daises and proclaiming themselves to be heroes. It comes out most when a tragedy occurs.

There used to be three choices of what to do after a natural disaster, mass shooting, or terrorist incident:

1. Cut a check to a charity.
2. Go there like Sean Penn with a shotgun and a paddle.
3. Shut the fuck up.

Now, we've added:

4. Post on social media, feel proud, and proclaim yourself a hero but accomplish nothing.

The algorithm in the head of someone who chooses number four is basically this: "I don't want to go to Haiti and get tetanus. I don't want to cut a check, because I like my money. What if I just hit Twitter and tear a comedian a new asshole over a joke?"

The easiest way to do number four is to jump on some trending hashtag, spit out a cliché that shows you are on the right side of the issue, and then get back to binge-watching Netflix.

Here are just a couple of the stupidest examples from the past few years:

**#OscarsSoWhite:** I love the idea of all the actors and directors who got on board that hashtag complaining about the lack of diversity of the nominees when *they're the Academy*. It's not like the crew voting on the Oscars are the people in MAGA caps at a Florida Trump rally. If you don't think the Oscars are diverse enough, vote for more diversity.

**#WeAreCecil:** The people who live in Africa where Cecil the lion was shot don't give a fuck, but the yentas in Orange County, California, were aghast. This is the definition of a liberal, when the feelings overtake the facts. The human body count from issues people don't want to discuss—like black gang violence in Chicago or murders committed by illegal immigrants in Texas, Arizona, and California—far outweighs the animal death toll from trophy hunting. But it was an easy issue to take a stance on and feel good about.

I would love to build a time machine for the express purpose of going back to 2014, about eleven months before the dentist who killed Cecil went on safari, and say to him, "Guess what is going to be the biggest Halloween costume this coming year."

"I don't know, Wonder Woman?"

"Nope. You."

"What? I'm a dentist from Roanoke, Virginia."

"Yes, and you are going to be the biggest Halloween costume of 2015." As he asks why, I would just cackle and fire up the time machine to leave his blown mind to sort it out.

**#BoycottPeterRabbit:** This one forced Sony Pictures to issue an apology for a scene in *Peter Rabbit* in which the bunnies throw blackberries at the farmer after finding out he is allergic to them. He collapses before injecting himself with an EpiPen. This spawned the aforementioned hashtag and an online petition that I have to assume was sponsored by a group called Future Pussies of America. Who are these people who have the energy to write earnestly that this promotes "allergy bullying"? Even worse, Sony responded, "Food allergies are a serious issue. Our film should not have made light of Peter Rabbit's archnemesis, Mr. McGregor, being allergic to blackberries, even in a cartoonish, slapstick way. We sincerely regret not being more aware and sensitive to this issue, and we truly apologize." Again, a forced apology is only about shutting you up or getting a blowjob sometime in the future. It means nothing.

Of course, the grandmama of them all is #MeToo, but that warrants its own chapter.

I get why this happens. Dr. Drew was recently talking about getting involved in some hashtag discussion and receiving a lot of positive feedback. He liked it. As any addiction specialist should, he knew he was feeling high. Human beings are wired to alleviate pain. Pain is a signal that something needs to change. Like walking on a broken ankle, it hurts because you're making it worse. Well, there's a human need to be with other humans, to feel safe in our tribe. Our tribe is now on Twitter. So, we watch what we say to avoid the pain of taking shit on Twitter, and we join in on the groupthink—aka hashtags and trending topics—to feel like we're part of something bigger than ourselves.

This problem is only going to get worse. It's a feedback loop. The less employable you are, the more time you have to be on the internet complaining about stuff and making yourself look like a hero. A real hero would be out there doing something, or at least working and paying taxes. You assholes with your hemp Priuses parked outside the Starbucks where you're working on your shitty screenplays have nothing but time. How about this one that I hope trends after this book comes out? #GetTheFuckToWork

## The Cancer of Cancel Culture

The most dangerous form of social media misuse is so-called cancellation, when we dredge up high school photos, ancient interviews, or old social media posts of people years later, sometimes after they're dead, and "cancel" those people.

I hate that "Well what about...?" bullshit. We shouldn't be constantly punching at the rear-view mirror of life. Let's focus on what is happening now that we can do better with and what we can prepare for or prevent in the future. Responding to someone bringing up the issue of Muslim extremism with, "Well what about the Crusades?" accomplishes nothing other than making me stop listening to you.

Judging history by the standards of today is the most annoying habit of the left. Won't future generations in two hundred years look back at us now and say, "Adam Carolla *wasn't* gender-queer? Well, I shan't be watching his shows anymore! He was a monster!"? There's a lot of trashing of the founding fathers for being slave owners. The horrors of slavery are obvious to us now, but two hundred years ago that horror was common practice. At the time, you would have been an idiot not to own slaves. The only reason more people didn't is because they couldn't afford them. Slaves weren't seen as people; they were property, and who wouldn't want more property? How do you think our grandkids' grandkids will look at us paying Mexicans eleven dollars an hour to haul trash, put up concrete block walls, and dig ditches? In forty years, when we have robots doing all of the manual labor, how will history judge us for paying real people just above free? Slavery was free; what we're paying Mexicans now is just slightly more than that. Our current agreement with the most destitute people on the planet is, "You will toil in the hot sun all day, and at the end I will pay you enough to go buy a Filet-O-Fish." Do you think history is going to be kind to this? Yet, there are plenty of "progressives" like my mom and grandmother, who happily pay gardeners and laborers as little as they can afford to without getting arrested. While they were watching *Roots* and preaching about the evils of slavery they were basically practicing "slavery lite."

Last year, someone dug up and posted on Twitter a 1971 *Playboy* interview with John Wayne. (Are you sitting down?) He said some racist and homophobic shit. Yes, in 1971, "the Duke" used the word "faggot" and said we should have taken the land from the Indians. Can you believe it? The star of *Stagecoach* and *Fort Apache*! My world is upside down. It's nuts that we're now living in a time when dead celebrities still need a PR team. Some post-mortem publicist is going to need to get the estate of John Wayne to okay a CGI avatar with Rich Little doing the voice to go on *The View* to say, "Howdy, Pilgrim. I like pilgrims of all races and sexual and gender orientations, and I sincerely apologize for my hurtful words in 1971."

Why are we burning calories being offended by stuff from the past? I feel like I can watch a Roman Polanski movie, listen to a little Michael Jackson, and eat at a Mario Batali restaurant despite their actions. All I'm asking is that we have some context. Henry Ford was a well-documented anti-Semite. He distributed anti-Jewish conspiracy literature to all his employees. He manufactured the planes test-piloted by the second-biggest anti-Semite, Charles Lindberg. But when the rubber hit the road, literally, in World War II, we would not have defeated Hitler had Ford not built Willow Run and turned his other factories into "the arsenal of democracy." That's what's important—actions, not thoughts or feelings.

Of course, this digital dredging bullshit also led to Kevin Hart's stepping down as host of the Academy Awards. When he didn't pass the left's purity test because of some ten-year-old "homophobic" jokes, we ended up with a host-free, all woke, no joke Oscars.

Then there was a friend of my show, James Gunn. He was a guest before he ever hit it big with the *Guardians of the Galaxy* franchise and is someone I'll always respect and wish well, which is why I was extra pissed when some conservative blogger took umbrage at his anti-Trump stance and busted out the shovel to start digging for indignation and created an unnecessary issue that got him booted from directing the third film in the series. The twisted sensibility that led to a great movie franchise is also the twisted sensibility that wrote jokes about rape and pedophilia. He's edgy. He's like the straight John Waters except with talent. I want him going to the line and occasionally past it. That's what being an artist is. Fortunately, this digital indignation incident had a happy ending when his cast and his fans stood up for him and Disney rehired him.

He was briefly canceled but got clemency at the last minute. The problem is, we have no standard for what constitutes a hanging offense. There are plenty of people who have done a lot worse than James Gunn, or Roseanne Barr, who didn't get canceled.

We're all treated to Shaq doing commercials for Papa John's Pizza because the company's founder, John Schnatter, accurately talked about Colonel Sanders using the N-word while on a conference call and was then dimed out by his own "crisis manager." He lost a multimillion-dollar company he built himself in 1984 out of a broom closet with $1,600 he got from selling his Camaro. Yet Papa John Phillips of the Mamas and the Papas was having a sexual relationship with his own daughter, and "California Dreamin'" is still in heavy rotation on every oldies station.

Again, this is chick-think. Fifty years ago, men weren't gossips who would tell you shitty things people said because they "just thought you should know." That was the domain of housewives talking over coffee while their husbands were at work. Now all the young dudes carry the news that no one needs to know on an iPhone in their skinny-jeans pocket. The tattletale pussy who goes through James Gunn's Twitter timeline to let you know he made some gay jokes a decade ago is no better than the sitcom nosy neighbor peeping over the fence to get some gossip to spread around the neighborhood. Fuck you, Mrs. Kravitz. ( Q Google It )
**bit.ly/ESA-Kravitz**

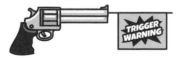

This one is addressed to the fifty-one-year-olds talking about getting off Twitter because it's bumming them out. I hear many people talking about taking "social media vacations," especially in the Trump era. I hear adult males talk about being bummed out all day and crying in front of their children because of something they saw posted online. I know I just spent a whole chapter complaining about social media, but I never said we should get rid of it or that I couldn't handle it. Like every problem in society, I want to look at it, figure out how we can make it better, and make a couple of bucks complaining about it on a podcast or in a book. My wiring is good when it comes to this stuff. I use Twitter like I use all tools—for the right job and only when necessary. No one can make me feel a certain way about myself. I give a tweet as much credence as something muttered by a homeless guy. I'm going to be in charge of how I feel about myself. People will tweet me horrible shit like, "I feel sorry for your wife and daughter." Okay, fuckface. I'll pass that along to them as soon as they get out of the Jacuzzi, the one that's in the master suite, not the one attached to the pool. Don't shed any tears for them.

Say "Just saw Adam Carolla doing stand-up…" and I'll tune in. But if you jump right to "Adam is the unfunniest fuck on the planet, and here's why…" I'm not going to listen to the remainder of the sentence. If your intention is to get me or my mind to change, then you have failed miserably. When you start calling everyone Hitler, the targets of your ire tune out. It's too extreme. We need to be able to understand intention and not be so reactive. We aren't going to change the way we communicate, but we can change the way we feel. The social media horse has left the barn. If you can't handle it, you're fucked. This is mental weakness. How precarious is your self-esteem that one tweet can knock it off its shelf? If people being mean to each other or saying things you disagree with can get you that depressed, you don't need to get off Twitter, you need to go on Zoloft.

All of that said, Twitter and other social media posts shall be the records of the time period when our civilization collapsed, which, at the rate we're going, should be at about noonish on Saturday. When the archeologists, or aliens, come here later to study our ruins, I just wish I could be around to see them be amazed at the stupid shit we cared about and how much time we spent tweeting at windmills.

# Chapter 6

# Academia Nuts

I didn't go to an Ivy League school. I was put on academic probation at Valley College, a public community college in L.A. My ivy league was my first construction job pulling ivy off the side of a house in Silverlake. It was pretty much spot-welded to the stucco. I'd yank it, and it would come off with a pop. A plume of fifty years' worth of rat shit and soot from settled freeway smog would shake off and pour into my lungs. I'd lug the ivy to the dumpster and do it again until I wanted to kill myself. It was a Sisyphean task. (I had to look that one up. I thought "Sisyphus" was an insult combining "sissy" and "puss.")

So, while I'm not fully qualified to talk about free speech on campuses, I'm going to speak freely about it anyway.

We had a saying when I was a lad that the kids today need to start using again: "Sticks and stones may break my bones, but names can never hurt me." On college campuses nowadays, kids have decided that names can hurt. Much like the correction cultists I talked about earlier, campus language cops have changed the definition of the word "dangerous." They say the points Ben Shapiro makes about abortion, the Black Lives Matter movement, and the Israeli-Palestinian conflict, for example, are not things they disagree with but rather are "dangerous." I would posit that there are no dangerous words. I'm pretty sure George Carlin and his seven dirty words would agree with me. It goes back to the mentality of victimhood permeating our culture. These college kids are looking for a victimizer to fit the narrative in which they are victims. In comes big, bad Ben Shapiro with his hurtful and "dangerous" rhetoric. Rhetoric can't harm. It's right there in the term. Ever hear of a rhetorical question? It's defined as "a question asked for the sake of persuasive effect rather than as a genuine request for information...." It's about making a point, not about inciting violence. Even if people were engaging in racist, bigoted, or homophobic hate speech, that should be the easiest to shoot down, right? Let's say Ben Shapiro's message actually is "Black people are inferior." That's an easy argument to defeat. It's not too difficult to win an intellectual argument with a Klansman. Klansmen come armed with a burning cross but not a lot of facts. And it's hard to hear them through the hoods. The problem is that Ben's points are nuanced and backed up with statistics. If he was just spouting racist tropes, he'd fare as well in his arguments as Archie Bunker did against Meathead. But, rather than enter a debate they know they'll lose, people on campuses say Ben Shapiro is spouting "dangerous hate speech," get virtue points for standing up to it, call themselves brave, and avoid getting humiliated by Ben.

You know who is brave? Ben fucking Shapiro. He doesn't say what he says from the safety of a podcast studio. He wades into angry mobs on college campuses or at Black Lives Matter rallies, stands his ground, and says his piece. This is a diminutive Jew. He's the one with a target on his yarmulke.

For a group that crows incessantly about diversity, how about the diversity of ideas? I'm much more interested in having a variety of brains on campuses than a variety of skin colors. There's hell to pay on a campus now if the faculty, student body, and guest speakers don't look like one of those fake multiracial bands or groups at rooftop parties you see in beer and credit-card ads. When it comes to multiculturalism, it seems to not include my culture, which is sane people.

There are campus officials with genuinely straight faces saying things like, "I'm all for free speech. I defend everyone's right to free speech. I just need to hear what it is first so I can vet it to see if it's allowable or not." They green-light only the stuff that they agree with. This is Harvard and Yale, not the Wally Thorpe School of Trucking. Shouldn't you have more intellectual honesty if you're a top intellectual institution?

People are getting sick of this crap. A study shows that alumni are not donating as much to their respective alma maters, because they see this campus cowardice and think about when their protests were for shit that actually mattered, like Vietnam, feminism, and civil rights. This is the generation that saw their friends gunned down by the National Guard at Kent State. They couldn't give a fuck about you pussies crying into your stuffed animals because Milo Yiannopoulos is defending Donald Trump, so they're putting their checkbooks away.

In 2016 at DePaul University, Milo was attacked onstage by a group of Black Lives Matter protesters. Security personnel did nothing, because they were scared. They didn't want the hassle and negative attention of taking black protesters off the stage. If someone were to rush the stage while Jon Stewart was doing a set, security would be on it. But because it was Milo contradicting the idea of systemic racism, they turned a blind eye.

I don't get the idea of using aggression and violence against conservative speakers on campus. I think that behavior kind of proves their point. I would understand violence breaking out over a difference of opinion in a bar or on a naval vessel. But on a college campus, you're supposed to be intellectual, able to hear differing opinions and debate them. The dumbos I grew up with are the ones who swing broken beer bottles at people and inanimate objects they don't like. ("That mailbox is giving me the stink eye.") You should be wielding your ideas, not pepper spray. Why get so agitated? Just move on.

Here are a few events that took place at the University of California, Berkeley, in 2018 that I had my staff pull for the podcast. These are events I would never go to.

- Solidarity for Nicaragua: Caravan for Peace
- *Mother, Daughter, Sister* Film Screening and Panel on Sexual Violence in Myanmar
- Teaching About Dialect: Identity Variation and Power
- Identifying and Addressing Workplace Bullying

Actually, re: that last one, I would like to not only attend but preside. I'd flick the lights on and off once and say, "You're all worthless and weak. Now get the fuck out of here, pussies." Again, I'd never go to any of these events, but I would never try to interrupt or protest them either. If you don't agree with the topic, how about you just don't fucking go? Musical acts play campuses all the time. Let's take Duran Duran, for example. I find their music to be a macroaggression toward my ears. I am offended as a person with good taste in music. But if I were a student and found out that Duran Duran was playing my campus, I just wouldn't go. I wouldn't feel the need to protest or call in a bomb threat. I would simply go off campus, find a bar with some Elvis Costello in the jukebox, and get shitfaced.

Administrators coddle protesters and encourage this nonsense. In 2016, one college went so far as to remove an incredibly incendiary, violence-inciting symbol of hate. We sane people know it as the American flag. It was at Hampshire College in Amherst, Massachusetts. (Go Fightin' Pussies!) It seems that after Trump's election, some students were so triggered that they lowered the flag to half-staff in protest. The campus authorities (and I use that word loosely) kept it at half-staff until the next night, when it was burned. Rather than deal with the fuckwads who *committed arson*, they took down the flag entirely. The college president said the students who burned it saw the flag as "a powerful symbol of fear they've felt all their lives because they grew up in marginalized communities, never feeling safe." Back to the victimization identity.

If you traveled back in time to 1963, interrupted a Don and Betty Draper–esque couple eating a homemade casserole, enjoying a martini, and watching Ed Sullivan, and told them, "In the future we'll have something called an iPhone. It will be a television, a telephone, a map, a calculator, a record player, a camera, and a butler, all in one device the size of the pack of Lucky Strikes you're currently smoking at the dinner table, and there will also be a college campus in *America* that finds it too controversial to fly the *American* flag," the thing they would be most confused about is the flag part. "Time machine? Sure. iPhone? Makes sense; we're on the cusp of the space age. No flag on campus? Shut the fuck up, future man!"

## My Case against the Safe Space

Where campuses really get absurd is with "safe spaces." For those of you unfamiliar with this term, congratulations. A so-called safe space is an area for students to escape to with stuffed animals, counselors, coloring books, and support animals for when Jordan Peterson or some other monster comes to campus. Think *Romper Room*, except instead of four-year-olds, it's for nineteen-year-olds who think like four-year-olds.

Many of my longtime podcast listeners know about my plan to round up deadbeat dads. It would be like one of those sting operations in which the cops get a list of guys with outstanding warrants, send them each a letter that they've won a jet ski, then, when the guys show up to claim their prize, tackle them and throw them in the zip ties. My idea is to rent out the L.A. Coliseum for a day and hang a big sign: "Free Cockfights for Raiders Fans." Anyone who shows up would inevitably be a tax-dodging deadbeat dad. Well, I finally found my white-collar version of this. We'll set up fake safe spaces on campuses and, when Ben Shapiro or Ann Coulter comes to speak, anyone who enters gets a butterfly net thrown over them and is shipped down to Mexico.

There's also this version of it: in the fall of 2019, the University of Kansas offered a class called Angry White Male Studies. I'm pretty sure what you're holding right now could be the fucking textbook. My idea was that anyone who signed up for that class would get intercepted on their way in, hogtied, thrown in a crate, and shipped to whatever god-forsaken country Boko Haram is in. See how well they fare with the angry males there. I'm sure it'd be a fuckload less well than in the United States. (By the way, "Whiter Shade of Pale" is my favorite song by Boko Haram.)

Before you start busting out the "white privilege" bullshit, let me throw a quote at you on the topic of safe spaces. "I don't want you to be safe ideologically. I don't want you to be safe emotionally. I want you to be strong.... I'm not going to pave the jungle for you. Put on some boots and learn how to deal with adversity." That was Van Jones, Obama appointee and civil rights leader.

There are only two options when it comes to feeling threatened by a conservative speaker on campus. You're either an outright liar causing trouble for no reason, or you actually feel threatened, in which case you need Prozac, not protection. With the recent spate of Uber drivers abducting young women outside college bars, it's worth bearing in mind what an actual attack on campus is. Ben Shapiro sharing some words from the Old Testament or Jordan Peterson citing statistics about gender roles is not an attack.

This is about the death of authority. The inmates are running the asylum. When you're mad at your dad and you eventually move out and onto a campus, the dean becomes Dad. If these whiny little bitches, and I include males in the term "bitches," still lived at home, they would be protesting the pot roast. "No Justice, No Meat!" Do you think you could pull any of these people out of one of these protests and ask, "How's your relationship with your dad?" and have them say, "It's great; I respect him very much"? Fuck no.

The adults are on college campuses to impart information, thoughts, and ideas to kids, and the kids are there to absorb those things. That would be all well and good if there were no biases. Imagine if every professor on every college campus were vegan. History teachers would be educating about the settling of the West and, while talking about the buffalo, they would trickle in the fact that all animals are sentient creatures who deserve to live.

There's no way their veganism would never bleed in. So when the kids who go to Vegan University come home on break and Mom busts out the pork chops, the kid is going to say, "Meat is murder." It's indoctrination.

I wish professors were vegan. They're something worse: socialists. Think about the profession they've chosen, from your Ivy League college professors down to your average public school teachers. All the blowhards who call themselves educators are using that title to cover up what they really are—people who want nothing to do with the competition of the private sector. Of course there are exceptions, like Cornel West and Alan Dershowitz, who have parlayed being professors into lucrative enterprises off campus, but for every one of them there are nine hundred dipshits who tried and failed to educate me. We have a new world order in which everyone has eighteen jobs in their lifetime. You know who doesn't? Teachers. Because they love kids? Hell no. They want summers off and to retire at fifty-five with a fat pension. They can't teach capitalism, financial literacy, competition, the free market, grit, or integrity any more than a vegan professor can teach how to gut an elk. Yet we wonder why every kid leaves high school not knowing how to manage a bank account, and leaves college drowning in debt.

Teachers avoid preaching about these subjects because they've avoided practicing them their whole lives. An energetic, driven, creative person like me couldn't tolerate working at the same place for thirty-seven years. "Academics," on the other hand, love the idea of tenure. There's no competition, and they get to suck on the teat, often of taxpayers, and avoid potential failure in the real world. That's the real safe-space crisis on campus. Whether they know it or not the teachers and administrators are hiding out on campuses protecting themselves from competing and passing that retarded ideology on to every student they encounter. Can you imagine the amazing generation of entrepreneurs and businesspeople that would come out of a college run by the cast of *Shark Tank*? Instead, we've got lazy people who hate this country and are willing to ruin generations for the security of tenure.

These college professors and administrators are scared of the kids. Students used to be students. Now they're customers. As far as these colleges go, the customer is always right. The colleges are essentially babysitters who show up and are told that the kids are supposed to eat a healthy dinner, read until ten p.m., and then go to bed. As soon as the parents leave, the babysitter says, "What do you want to do?" and the kids reply, "We want to stay up until three a.m., eat jelly beans, and watch bootleg porn." The babysitter says, "Okay, let's take a vote." The kids' hands shoot up, and the ayes have it. The babysitter's job is to say no, not take a vote. But these people are trying to win a popularity contest and avoid work. They don't want to deal with these little shits.

Think I'm being hyperbolic about students' being kids demanding jelly beans? Last year the students at Sarah Lawrence College took over the campus and staged sit-ins in administrative buildings due to some serious, serious concerns. They had a list of demands. Here are a few of them.

*Sarah Lawrence must commit to actualizing the value that housing is a human right. The college must provide winter housing to students at no charge. The housing must include a communal kitchen with dry goods from the pantry for all students.*

And:

*Sarah Lawrence must commit to actualizing the value that no student go hungry. The college must commit to devising a food plan where every student has access to at minimum two meals a day, including weekends, school breaks and days when the college is closed due to weather. When dining options are closed on campus the college must provide free meals for students staying on campus including gluten-free, vegan, vegetarian, kosher and halal options.*

There were plenty of other demands, including "access to unlimited free therapy sessions" and "students of color should not be forced to resort to racist white professors in order to have access to their own history." (I would argue that it's a racist notion in and of itself to assume that a white professor is racist simply because he's white, but I could do a whole other chapter on that.) The point is that this is the breakdown of the rule of law. The first thread in the unraveling of the sweater of the rule of law was that parents stopped saying, "Because I said so." They started pulling up to the side of the bed to have a heart-to-heart with little Dylan about every issue. They opened a dialogue and simultaneously opened a can of worms. Those kids grew up, and now they're negotiating with every authority figure in their lives, whether it's campus administrators or cops.

You know who I blame for all of this? Hitler. Hear me out. The greatest generation went off to fight in World War II and came back traumatized. This is all about trauma. They saw their friends shredded by mortar fire. So, they went one of two ways, or alternated between the two. They shut down or got heavy-handed, usually with a little help from Jack Daniels. These men had shell shock, a.k.a. PTSD, so the babies they boomed when they got back stateside were raised either by checked-out, emotionally dead or distant dads, or by aggressive, angry, alcoholic dads. As a result, those kids hated authority figures. This was the generation at

Berkeley chanting, "Don't trust anyone over thirty" and patting themselves on the back for Woodstock because they managed to cobble together three days during which no one killed anybody. (I imagine if Woodstock had stretched to day five, it would have gone a little *Lord of the Flies* and they'd have killed and eaten Sha Na Na.) Their hatred of authority and the norm had an interesting ripple effect. They thought "out of the box" and became leaders in Silicon Valley and on college campuses. That's the point. The people in charge now were raised by tuned-out or heavy-handed dads; lost faith in the very idea of authority, even if they themselves are the authorities, and are letting the next generation of super-hippies run rampant all over our culture.

## Mr. Carolla Goes to Washington

I'm usually recognized in airports with the phrase "Hey, *Man Show*! Where are the Juggies?" But on July 27, 2017, I was recognized by Jim Jordan, the chair of—this is the actual title from the official government record—THE JOINT HEARING BEFORE THE SUBCOMMITTEE ON HEALTHCARE, BENEFITS AND ADMINISTRATIVE RULES AND THE SUBCOMMITTEE ON INTERGOVERNMENTAL AFFAIRS OF THE COMMITTEE ON OVERSIGHT AND GOVERNMENT REFORM, HOUSE OF REPRESENTATIVES, ONE HUNDRED FIFTEENTH CONGRESS.

Not bad for a kid who never took an algebra class and had a 1.75 GPA.

To this day, I don't know why I was asked to be at the hearing. It was the same way I got invited to do *Dancing with the Stars*. I didn't plan on doing it, I didn't ask for it, I just got a call, felt a twinge of fear, and said yes (like one should do with all fears). Most of what Congress does is act like they do something, so I was under no illusions that anything I had to say to them would lead to anything. It was nothing more than an exercise in "Well, I get to say that I did that."

I was made aware of it two weeks in advance. I was a shitty student in high school, and that gene stays with you your entire life. I knew that I was going to have five minutes to read a prepared statement. That sentence shows the problem; it has my two least favorite words—"read" and "prepare." Like any D student, I procrastinated. I knew I needed five minutes, but I also knew I had a five-hour flight to D.C. to get my shit together.

I got drunk and passed out on the plane. There was no prep.

Arriving there was surreal. I emotionally downplay everything so that I won't get overwhelmed by it. In this case, I had just assumed it wasn't *Congress* Congress, but like Junior Congress in a mobile trailer up on blocks behind the real Capitol building. Like what we referred to as the Dummy Cottages behind North Hollywood High for the students, including many of my friends, who went to the "alternative" school. In my mind this was the congressional equivalent of the Daytime Emmys. The real varsity squad of the legislative branch couldn't possibly be consulting my ass. I was wrong. This was the real deal. There were giant domed buildings I had only ever seen on TV and in movies. I was thinking like the Talking Heads song "Once in a Lifetime." "You may ask yourself. Well, how did I get here?" What the fuck was the near dropout from North Hollywood High doing in the same building where FDR delivered his "a date which will live in infamy" speech after Pearl Harbor? Plus, I was being filmed for *No Safe Spaces*, so there was added pressure. Striking out is bad, but if there's no one in the stands at the Toledo Mud Hens ballpark, it doesn't hurt as much as if you're at a full Dodger Stadium. The congressional hearing room was stately. There was a lot of clean blue carpet and polished white marble, and there were a lot of oil paintings of dead white guys.

As soon as I got to the hearing room and looked at the Murderers' Row of intellectuals I somehow found myself in company with—Ben Shapiro, New York University law school professors, college presidents—my shitty student habits kicked into overdrive. I asked who was going first, because I didn't want it to be me. I needed some time to cram, and thought if one or two of these other blowhards went first, I could scribble down some notes and skate through. We sat down at the big mahogany desk with the nameplates, microphones, and water glasses. There were congressmen on a dais and witnesses in the chamber. This was real. This was on C-SPAN. I looked over at Ben Shapiro, who was sitting next to me. He had five and a half typewritten, all-caps, single-spaced pages. You could tell he had rehearsed. It was a minute a page. He was locked and loaded and ready to go. But technically, he had next to nothing, because he was next to me and I had nothing. The chick on my left from NYU Law had her stuff completely prepared in a neat leather binder. Meanwhile, I was looking down at a well-worn steno pad with a handful of words like "children," "future," "law & order," "Purell," "Chicano," "Dr. Drew," and "gravity" misspelled, with arrows, numbers, and cross-outs. It looked like a Chinese road map. Following Ben Shapiro in congressional testimony is like following an Indian kid in a spelling bee.

It got real when they made us swear in. Usually I just swear, but I never swear to tell the truth, the whole truth, and nothing but the truth. In keeping with the whole truth, I present below my uncut, unprepared remarks before the committee.

*Thank you. It's an honor to be asked to speak in front of you all. First, just a quick piece of business. Do we get to keep these pads? This is going to be huge. And not that I'm going to, but what do you reckon they'll get on eBay? I'm not saying I'm going to, but it's just pure curiosity. I'm not as eloquent as Mr. Shapiro. I sort of speak in beats and off the top of my head, and I've written a few down for you all today. First off, I come from a very blue-collar background. I grew up in North Hollywood, California. My dad was a schoolteacher, and my mom received welfare and food stamps and told me very importantly when I was young when I asked her if she would get a job, she said, "And lose my welfare benefits? No, thank you," which taught me a very valuable lesson, which is never to listen to my mom. All right. I ended up being a carpenter and then a boxing instructor and met Jimmy Kimmel when I taught him to box for a morning zoo stunt and eventually made my way onto TV and radio. In the early days of my career, I toured the country with Dr. Drew when we were on Loveline together, a syndicated radio program also on MTV, and we must have played one hundred college campuses with nary a word of negativity and no safe spaces and no stuffed animals being handed out, simply went there, said our piece. Many controversial ideas were exchanged, and that's just what they were, exchanged, and then we got our paychecks and went home. And fifteen years later, I went out with Dennis Prager, a conservative talk show host, and attempted to do a show at Cal State Northridge, where my mother was an actual graduate from with a Chicano studies degree, believe it or not. So, she's rolling in dough about now. And they pulled the plug on it. They gave us no good reason why we couldn't speak there, and we actually had to get attorneys involved to go back and speak at a later date. We're talking a lot about the kids, and I think they're just that, kids. We are the adults, and I don't think we are doing the children—I mean, these are eighteen- and nineteen-year-old kids that are at these college campuses. They grew up dipped in Purell, playing soccer games where they never kept score, and watching Wow!*

*Wow! Wubbzy! and we're asking them to be mature. We need the adults to start being the adults. Studies have shown that if you take people and you put them in a zero-gravity environment like astronauts, they lose muscle mass, they lose bone density. We're taking these kids in the name of protection, we're putting them in a zero-gravity environment, and they're losing muscle mass and bone density. They need to live in a world that has gravity. When you—you need to expose your children to germs and dirt in the environment to build up their immune system. Our plan is put them in a bubble, keep them away from everything, and somehow they'll come out stronger when they emerge from the bubble. Well, that's not happening. Children are the future, but we are the present and we're the adults and we need to act like it. And I feel that what's going on, on these campuses is, we need law and order. We need to bring back law and order, but I think if we just had order, we wouldn't need law. So, could we just bring back order, and could the faculty and administration on these campuses act like faculty and administration, and, most importantly, adults who are in charge of these kids who need some gravity in their life? Thank you.*

A Q&A session followed in which I was able to be a little more off-the-cuff. I had a couple good comebacks, points, and one-liners, but I think this was the best of them. Congressman Jim Jordan asked me if I was involved in hate speech on campus. I rebutted that no I was not but that I did make jokes. I then proceeded to ask Congressman Raja Krishnamoorthi if they charged him extra for his nameplate like they do for vans at the car wash.

## Don't Get Fresh, Men: Campus Rape Culture

The folks on the left claim that one in five women is raped at college. But you know those lefties are lying. Here's how. Because those same people have started savings accounts to send their thirteen-year-old girls to Rape University, or God forbid, Rape State. It's like people saying fifty-three thousand Americans die yearly of secondhand smoke. It's a lie, but it's a lie for a good cause. Even Biden got in on the action when he was VP, parroting that one-in-five statistic. Except that stat was gathered from an anonymous online survey at a college campus, and the authors of the study arbitrarily determined what constituted "unwanted sexual contact."

I thought campuses were the land of safe spaces? I don't understand how the most liberal establishments on the planet are also simultaneously the rapiest places on earth. Every left-leaning celebrity in L.A. worries about two issues: rape culture on campuses and rising sea levels. Yet they're all shipping their daughters off to college and moving to Malibu.

Fortunately, my daughter is a Carolla and probably won't be college material, so I don't have anything to worry about. Unless she does go to college, is as shitty a student as I was, and ends up there for eight years and thus has a 40 percent chance of being raped. Shit, now that I think about it, my mom went to L.A. Valley College for, like, sixteen years, so she was probably raped 147 times.

## 2 Lie Crew

I can't talk about celebrities sending their daughters to college without taking a little detour into the Lori Loughlin/Felicity Huffman college admissions scandal. If you're reading this section twenty years in the future, hopefully you're laughing at how stupid this "scandal" was.

First off, wouldn't it have been easier to hire an Olympic rowing coach and actually get their daughters on the crew team?

They shelled out hundreds of thousands of dollars in Photoshop-ping services, fake letters, and bribes. Crew is the easiest sport to fake. All you have to do is not be fat. No one is ever going to question you. "You don't seem like coxswain material to me. Quick, what's the difference between sculls and sweeps?" It also proves that no one gives a fuck about that sport. No one ques-tioned it. And there's definitely a racial component. If someone had tried to pretend that their spindly honky of a kid was joining the USC football team, that'd be a little bit of a tell. That actually may be a real example of white privilege, being able to pretend to be on a crew team. The only crew a black guy has ever been on is a work crew.

I thought the grandstanding by police when Felicity Huffman and Lori Loughlin were taken into custody was ridiculous. These are middle-aged actresses, not El Chapo. Do we really need the full *Raid on Entebbe* treatment? How about the poor neighbors who were awakened at six a.m. by the SWAT team screeching up and loading clips into AR-16s? It wasn't like Felicity Huffman was going to pull a full Ruby Ridge and go down in a blaze of glory. These actresses might have money, but they're not flight risks. The cops should have just hung outside with the TMZ photographers and when Felicity and Lori walked out to go to Starbucks flashed them a badge, taken them in, processed them, and then put ankle bracelets on them to keep them at home. The only people who would want this scenario more than me would be *New York Post* so they'd have the opportunity to use the following Lori Loughlin headline: "Full House Arrest."

I have no ire about these people. They're doing what rich people do. Our society has givers and takers. These people are earners. They don't need to be put behind bars. They don't need to be made examples of. I want them out earning money to pay taxes. I'm much more worried about the guys who randomly coldcock Hasidic Jews in New York than Felicity Huffman. The guy who threw the cinder block at Reginald Denny when he was lying on the ground during the L.A. riots is much scarier to me than the chick from *Desperate Housewives*. We don't need these actresses in cages. How many of the people who acted outraged were affected by this? Zero. So who are we protecting by putting Aunt Becky in jail? No one. When Dr. Dre adds a new building to the campus of USC, his kid gets to go there and no one cares. But these women do it through back channels and we need to get our panties in a twist? Al Gore's four kids all went to Harvard. Are you telling me that it had nothing to do with Daddy's position? What's the difference between peddling influence and peddling money? They're both commodities that the college is willing to let dumb kids into their school to have. Who cares?

I don't know why we were so shocked that two famous actresses bent the rules to get their kids into prestigious schools. Famous actors are famously narcissistic. But if we broaden it to the other well-to-do folk caught up in the scandal, there is that common theme. In the mind of a narcissist, their kid is an extension of them. They put on an expensive Rolex because the Rolex is an extension of them. Or they drive a Rolls-Royce. That's an extension of them. A symbol that they've made it. Something that grabs attention from the common man to let the common man know they're better. Well, what's the difference between their kid and a Rolls-Royce? Their kid and a mansion? Their kid and fancy jewelry? Their kid is a greater expression of them than the watch or the luxury sedan. Having their kids get into Stanford or USC gave these parents bragging rights to make themselves look good, no different than the Rolls or Rolex. These parents weren't treating their kids as human beings but as accessories.

We all hate the pageant mom who takes her five-year-old, spray-tans her, gives her Tammy Faye Bakker makeup and lash extensions, and says, "Oh, that's what she wants to do." What's the difference if you really think about it? We might look at the college mom as healthy because the kid ends up on the campus of USC, and the pageant mom as unhealthy because the kid ends up on the pole at Spearmint Rhino, but what motivates the decision comes from the same place. So, either the mom is in the audience at the Little Miss Sunshine pageant applauding for her kid and thus herself, or the mom is at the Stanford graduation doing the same thing. One is trailer trash and the other is educated and wealthy, but either way, all roads lead to narcissism. The greatest irony is that the Stanford mom would never stop making fun of the pageant mom, but they're narcissistic sisters from another mister.

The real reason this scandal caught fire is because it was about the "haves" and the "have nots" and fed into that narrative that's so rampant on college campuses and in society in general. Let me tell you something. It's not about the "haves" and the "have nots." It's about the "works" and the "work nots."

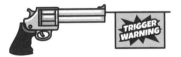

To all of you reading this who are thinking about going to college, especially community college, a.k.a. junior college, a.k.a. high school with ashtrays, just don't. It's not worth your money or time. We're all on to your game, even if you aren't.

As I mentioned, and as is now hilariously noted for all time in the congressional record, my mom was a Chicano studies major at L.A. Valley College, a two-year college, for over ten years, while hammering welfare checks. She and many of my friends were ticking the box for "going to college," but what they were really doing was hiding out from life. It's a great plan: take a few units at a junior college—it barely costs anything—and say, "I'm taking classes at the college" so people will nod and say, "Oh, good for you." Meanwhile, they don't know that you're taking the same pottery class for the third semester in a row.

The ruse with you nineteen-year-olds is that you're going to take a few courses at the local junior college and get the requirements out of the way before transferring to Brown or Yale. Bullshit. You were a horrible student at seventeen when you were barely hanging on in high school. Do you think something changed at eighteen and a half? When you got the right to vote and buy cigarettes, you also magically became a brainiac? You're going to show up late for class, get put on probation, say the teacher has it out for you, appeal it, and, because the school wants your money (usually taxpayer-subsidized in some way), begin your second lap of this retarded race to nowhere.

Face it, this is a place for you to hang out between failing in high school and getting the fuck to work or going into the military. It's a two-year hall pass to crash in your parents' basement, sleep in, eat their food, and pretend like you're doing something before they get sick of your ass and the indentation it's making in their sofa, and you get a job at Applebee's.

Until about age twenty-four, you can hustle that Three-Card-Monte. The version of this for those of you who are twenty-four to ninety-four is working the "continuing education" angle. You hide in plain sight without a bunch of people asking you why you're not working and contributing to society.

We need to take a giant rake to all these places every three and a half years. If you can't get through the two-year program in two years, you're out. All the people like my mom and a young dumb me and my buddies need to get flushed out of there like the shit from one of Gwyneth Paltrow's colonics.

Even if you were truly interested and motivated, these colleges offer way too many classes. They can't possibly all be taught well. Plus, there's no way community colleges are paying for high-quality teachers. I bet half the teachers graduated from those junior colleges within the past four years themselves. It's like the Cheesecake Factory. The menu has way too many items, and I doubt the "chefs" there do a dynamite pad Thai, braised short ribs, and linguine and clams. Everything is mediocre, and no one leaves satisfied.

Going to junior college is methadone for the real effort of turning your life around. How about instead of using the thin veil of "going to college" as covering fire for not going anywhere in life, you pound the pavement, even if it's the virtual pavement of Indeed or ZipRecruiter, get a job or learn a trade, and actually move ahead.

I'm making only one exception—Asian nursing students. They've been preparing for that career their whole lives and don't need anything beyond that LPN certificate. If this is you, don't waste your time or money on anything else. Best wishes on your two-year junior college journey. I'll see you at the urgent care.

# Chapter 7

## Sick of #MeToo? Me Too.

Before you tear me a new asshole for what I'm going to write in this chapter, let me begin with a preemptive strike. I'm going to stick my neck out and speak the difficult truth. I am against rape. There, I've said it, and I can't take it back. It was uncomfortable, but I'm a brave, brave hero.

It's fucking ridiculous that I even felt the need to do that, but ours is a society in which we put the "jerk" in "knee-jerk," and I couldn't trust that many folks wouldn't see the title of this chapter and instantly decide that I'm the misogynist from *The Man Show*, and that I must be pro–sexual assault. I'm not. To be clear: rape = bad.

What I am against is the collateral damage—not just the guys who had their careers ruined for nothing, but the bigger victims, context, reason, due process, and nuance.

I lay a lot of this at the feet of the "hashtag heroes" discussed previously, and their OCD—obsessive correction disorder. In changing the definitions of words, we have lost all sense of meaning and, simultaneously, our minds. One of the biggest examples of this is the word "rape." Ironically, we have raped the word "rape." Rape used to mean a guy with a switchblade snatching a woman in the park, dragging her behind the shrubs, and having his way with her while he held his hand over her mouth. Now, especially on college campuses, it has come to include any sexual encounter a woman regrets or was too drunk to remember, or any "unwanted sexual advance." If that's the definition, 100 percent of my hookups have been rape. I've never made a wanted sexual advance.

So, let's separate the rape wheat from the bad-date chaff. We'll start by taking a perp walk.

## The Perps

### Harvey Weinstein

Let's start with the creator of the perp waddle. I've hated this asshole since before they threw the big-and-tall handcuffs around his wrists. Seriously, fuck Harvey Weinstein. Not because of any sexual assaults he committed, but because of the raping he did of my wallet. His company bought my first independent movie, *The Hammer*, and I never saw a dime. He's famously been doing this to every independent filmmaker he's worked with for the past thirty years. Filmmakers make distribution deals to get paid after expenses, but the money "on the back end," as we say in show business—meaning after the film breaks even—never arrives. The distributors make up a bunch of "above the line" costs as a way to screw you out of profits. Weinstein notoriously turned this into an art form, and it was apparently his second favorite way to fuck people. The supposed print advertisements for *The Hammer* must have appeared exclusively at the airport in Beirut, because I never saw them.

I was thrilled to hear the tape of Weinstein pleading with the Italian model who wore a wire to one of their encounters not to leave and embarrass him. Not only because I wanted to hear that slob beg, but because it proved my point that no matter how much power a rich white guy has in Hollywood, the real power player is a twenty-three-year-old model. If you listen to that tape, you'll hear Harvey say "please" to her more than he did to every-one in the previous forty years. He spat out thirteen "pleases" in a minute and forty-five seconds.

It makes me wonder if his ex, Georgina Chapman, is looking for a new beau. There's a lot of upside. She's a rich, hot designer, of course, but more important, she was married to a hairy, lecherous pig. Any guy would look like a fantastic husband by comparison. She's not going to give you a lecture about throwing your socks next to the hamper. You can leave your omelet remnants stuck to the frying pan on the stove, and if she makes a peep you can shoot back, "Oh, did Harvey clean up the stove before or after he raped half of Hollywood?"

Apparently, Harvey's MO was to invite models and actresses to his room for "meetings," ask them for a massage, and then do his dirty deeds.

> **BTW** Allow me a few paragraphs, or pages, on massages. I have a lot of thoughts.
>
> First let's talk about the pressure. It can get too hard. I'm there to get rubbed and relaxed, not for the diminutive Asian woman to drop an elbow from the top turnbuckle. I did notice

that when my face is in that donut pillow, I can handle 30 percent more pain. They should have that at the dentist's office. The Asian woman works the knot under my shoulder like she's trying to push this thing the size of an apricot either up through my throat or down out of my ass. It's very confusing. Enya is playing while a lavender candle fills the room with a pleasant smell, and the lights are nap-worthy dim, but I feel like I'm getting put in zip ties by an overly aggressive cop. If I'm going to be tortured, the ambiance should change to fit the mood. Crank up some GWAR, put on a strobe light, and burn a candle that smells like "Hacksaw" Jim Duggan's crotch. ( Q Google It ) **bit.ly/ ESA-Hacksaw**

At some point around ten minutes in, they always ask, "How's the pressure?" I never have the courage to answer honestly. "Which pressure? The pressure not to fart? Because this is the longest I've ever been naked without farting. You've been kneading my viscera to the point where I think a little bit of Crest just came out of my asshole. Or the second pressure? The pressure not to roll over with a boner?" You know the massage table was invented by a woman, because they put the hole at the front for your nose but nothing in the middle for "Pinocchio's nose." I wouldn't necessarily use it, but it'd be good to know it's there. You'd lie down and the masseuse would tactfully use her foot to slide a cookie sheet under the hole, like when your stepdad had the El Camino leaking transmission fluid in the garage and your mom would place a drip tray to catch it. Again, I'm not saying I'd need it; I'm just saying it's a real hassle to replace one of those carpet squares.

There's also the timing aspect. You go to the massage place and put on a bathrobe. Then the masseuse comes in, tells you to hang it on the hook and get under the sheet, they'll be right outside. They're very coy about coming back into the room. Three minutes later they've got you greased up and are wedging their hands in places your wife has never touched. So what if you caught a glimpse of ass cheek while I was sliding under the sheet? Do you think if you came through the door a little prematurely, I'd say, "What's the meaning of this!!!!?? I signed up to be naked and manhandled with oil while you stare at my hairy ass crack. I *did not* sign up for you to glimpse my hip!" Just go out, count to ten Mississippi, and come back in. If you see a little side sack, it's on me for not getting under the sheet fast enough. And if you see the tip, then that's your tip.

And why the focus on hydration? I've had hundreds of massage therapists tell me after they're done that I need to drink water. I've never expended less energy in a darker place than this. Even when my arm flops off the table, you pull it back up for me, Ms. Massager. You've been sweating, squeezing this two-hundred-pound sack of shit known as Adam Carolla for an hour. You need the water, not me. The most water I am out is a little drool through the donut face pillow. You need some Pedialyte and a banana. You've been working your ass off working on my ass.

On to race and gender. I've never had a black massage therapist. There are more black people than Asians in the U.S. I've had Asians, gay men, even a blind guy, but never a black guy. I've never even seen one. I've never been sitting next to a pitcher of water with cucumber floating in it and had a woman of color come out and ask for her next client. There are certain jobs that attract certain races. White guys like putting out fires. For some reason Asian women are attracted to massage work. Some jobs feel like the past, and it probably bumps black folk to massage white people. We don't need balance in everything. The only time I've ever had a person of color put their hands on me not in anger was when I got a rubdown from my old black boxing trainer named "Scrap-Iron" (true name and true story).

I've had men and women give me massages, but there's always the awkward moment when you make the appointment and the booker asks, "Do you prefer a male or female?" and you have to pretend that you don't care. "Doesn't matter. I'm progressive. As long as the person has huge areolas and at least twenty feet of fallopian tubing, I'm cool." There's a double standard here that no one will admit to. Guys, if you survey them, would prefer their ladies get a massage from a lady. We pretend not to care, but if we had to choose, we'd always prefer that. First off, there have been a thousand porno movies that start with that scene. And I'm fucking positive our wives would prefer we get massages from other guys.

I'd like to point out a hypocrisy I've long complained about. We guys are completely okay with the idea of our wives or girlfriends getting totally naked and rubbed down in oil by a muscular male stranger on a weekly basis we're paying for, but flip the script and we get an aggressive lap dance, cum in our pants, and limp back to the hotel room in Vegas, and we're monsters. That's territory for divorce. At least I have part of my pants on when I get the lap dance. 😁

Of course, Harvey Weinstein went to "rehab" for "sex addiction." I want to run one of these places. If you manage a burn unit, you actually have to work. But if you operate the place Harvey went to, you're just giving him shelter from the paparazzi. How difficult can it be to let celebrities hide out on some nice Malibu property and eat gluten-free, non-GMO vegan meals for $50,000 a week?

My biggest takeaway from the Harvey Weinstein situation is that anyone can act. It's easy. No other job works this way. "Want to be a commercial airline pilot? No problem, just blow that fat Jew and we'll have you in the cockpit this afternoon." Operating a gantry crane? Blow that fat Jew. Interested in becoming a dental hygienist? Blow that Jew. Apparently knowing Oprah Winfrey and blowing Harvey Weinstein are the two ways you get a gig in this business.

The weirdest wrinkle in the whole story was the revelation that Harvey apparently likes to have at himself and finish in potted plants. Is this a thing? I've heard of "furries" but not *"fernies."* Did he have a ficus fetish? Good thing he's Jewish. God knows what he'd do to a Christmas tree.

### Mario Batali

Much like Harvey Weinstein, this is a disgusting guy who never could have gotten laid without having some power. In fact, I would make that the defense if I was his lawyer. Instead of putting Mario in a nice suit to make him look professional, or a cardigan to soften him up and make him sympathetic, I'd have him in a Ragu-stained wife-beater and cargo shorts (he can keep his trademark Crocs), and say, "Your honor. What are the chances this slob is going to get laid? Honestly, look at him. I rest my case."

## *Bill O'Reilly*

We don't know all the factors here. Pun intended. All we know is, Bill paid out thirty-two million dollars to settle a sexual harassment suit. All *I* know is that if you're a dude and you're exceptionally horny, you can't exist in this society anymore. If you cannot harness horniness and use it for good, you're in trouble. Everyone has cameras, Twitter accounts, and lawyers. Guys are going to have to change fast. You can't get male sexuality to go away. But God knows, we're trying. The fact is, some guys are just wired to be hornier than others. Doesn't matter if you're a god-fearing family man, being horny will trump it. You can't take super-horny guys and give them power and money. It's like giving that same power and money to a person who loves coke. They're going to kill themselves with it. I think that's the deal with Bill. He's a high-testosterone guy who got himself in a position to use it.

I'm not saying anything he did was okay. I don't even know what he actually did. Because of the pay-to-make-it-go-away part of this, we'll never know. But one thing for sure is that it really brought out the hypocrisy of many of my friends on the left. What about another notable Irishman, John F. Kennedy? Many of the MSNBC viewers who danced on O'Reilly's grave when he was fired from Fox News still venerate that degenerate. (Sorry to go all Nipsey Russell on you there.) Kennedy was forcing interns to blow cabinet members and advisors, but he still hasn't been "canceled." And for some reason, David Letterman also has gotten a pass despite having an intern-affair situation himself. Anyone who has righteous indignation about Bill O'Reilly should also be outraged about Dave.

Since we're on the topic, it gives me an excuse to tell a quick O'Reilly story. A big-time radio guy named Norm Pattiz is a friend. He owns PodcastOne, which distributes my show. Being a rich white guy from L.A., he has courtside season tickets for the Lakers. One time he invited me and Bill O'Reilly to sit with him on the floor. If you want to get laid in Hollywood, you don't sit next to Leo DiCaprio, you sit next to Bill. The next day I was on Bill's show and he was busting my chops. "Hey, Carolla, did you take any crap from your hipster Hollywood friends for sitting next to me at the Lakers game?" I shot back, "No, I just told everyone I was there with my dad."

### Louis C.K.

Before I dig into Louis C.K.'s particular peccadillos, let me say that he reminds me of another guy who probably could have been Me Too'd, too, but you wouldn't know it because he's not famous. When I started my syndicated morning show in 2006, our program director was a guy named Jack Silver. Jack had a tin ear for comedy, as evidenced by the fact that in our first year on the air, we had several comedians come through and Jack told us there were three he didn't want back on—Joel McHale, Zach Galifianakis, and Louis C.K. Until Louis's Me Too moment, could you imagine a more revered group of comedians? But to Jack they were persona non grata. You know what he did want? "More cooch talk." That's not hyperbole; that's a quote. I remember because he said it in a staff meeting after the show that led my newsgirl at the time, Teresa Strasser, to be so aghast that I suggested she was taking a rape shower in her mind.

We all know that when Louis is not doing stand-up, he's sitting down on the edge of a bed with someone watching him whack off. While he hasn't fully gotten back into the good graces of the comedy community, some people are willing to give him another shot, and after a Me Too forced sabbatical, Louis is back on the scene. Here's where my diabolical prank kicks in. When Louis does a theater show, he's up on a stage, which puts his crotch about six feet above the audience. Someone should buy ten front-row-center seats at his next gig and give them out to friends and family. The condition is that they each have to wear a hazmat suit, one of those yellow full-body suits like Bryan Cranston wore when he was cooking meth in *Breaking Bad*—right down to the respirator and goggles. As a comedian, Louis would appreciate the joke, and as a perv, he'd probably love the humiliation.

One more quick but important Louis story. Like many victimizers, he was once a victim himself. This was many years ago, and this is the first time this has ever come out in print. I wish I had spoken up sooner, but I have finally mustered the courage to speak. Years ago I was an eyewitness to Louis being sexually assaulted, and I did nothing.

One of the writers on *The Man Show* and *Crank Yankers*, comedian Jordan Rubin, would have midnight roller-disco parties, back when people were single and still had the will to live. He'd invite lots of different comedians he was friendly with. One evening we were roller-boogieing the night away at the roller rink. Louis had a sweat going, the kind of sweat that says, "I'm a guy who dances once every seven years at a wedding." We were in the locker room afterward, and Louis had his shirt off and was toweling down. From out of nowhere, my buddy Ray came up behind him, cupped his man tits, and jiggled them furiously. Louis was carrying a little extra weight at the time and was probably a B cup. To this day, Ray will defend himself by saying he thought it was "Roastmaster General" Jeffrey Ross (as if that somehow makes it better). The point is that after the world's worst reenactment of that Janet Jackson *Rolling Stone* cover photo, Louis was very upset. For a guy who likes to whack off in the presence of strangers, he was very uptight. Which is it, Louis? Do you have delicate sensibilities, or do you let your freak flag fly while you polish your flagpole in front of female underlings?

## Matt Lauer

Unlike Louis C.K., who will be able to make a comeback eventually, Matt Lauer won't. Not because what he did was worse or because the evidence against him is any less "he said, she said," but because he has no discernable talent to rely on. If you could do something, you could get back to doing it. But he does nothing. You couldn't shit-can Seth MacFarlane, Mike Judge, Howard Stern, or anyone else who brings something to the table. Matt is useless. Like Billy Bush, who I mentioned earlier in the Trump chapter, Matt Lauer is nothing but a handsome teleprompter. Look how quickly they replaced him. They just went for girl power and gave Hoda Kotb an extra glass of wine and an extra hour of time. When I heard that Matt's wife righteously left him and took half of his hundred-million-dollar net worth, I was furious. What the fuck had Matt Lauer ever done to deserve that kind of money? I'm sure there are any number of decently attractive local news guys who have the entire portfolio of Matt's skills—reading the news, not putting on weight, nodding and looking concerned when you're supposed to, and getting up at five thirty a.m.

> ( BTW ) We need a celebrity drop-off day like those events where you go to a high school parking lot and drop off paint cans, cleaning products, and car batteries. There're a lot of people we're just done with. Like Dennis Rodman. He's not getting rebounds or banging Carmen Electra anymore. We're kind of done with him, so let's recycle him. 😬

Back to Matt Lauer. Another case of incredible hypocrisy. NBC was so concerned with the victims of sexual abuse that they felt compelled to release the tape of Trump on the *Access Hollywood* bus. Certainly it had nothing to do with politics, right? But when Ronan Farrow came to NBC with an ironclad story about Harvey Weinstein, they suddenly lost interest in survivors of sexual trauma. Why? Harvey had the goods on Matt, their morning-show golden boy. They said their journalistic standard hadn't been met, that there wasn't enough evidence to run the Harvey story, and killed it. Yet they felt it was okay to run a tape of a presidential candidate from ten years earlier, recorded without his knowledge. Spare me the lecture on your journalistic ethics, NBC.

A quick couple of thoughts on the father of the Me Too movement, Ronan Farrow. Is he a eunuch? (Those of you who know how poorly I spell can only imagine how many attempts it took me to get that word right. My spell-check just kept coming back with the word "TILT." My computer started smoking, and the lights in my house dimmed.) Seriously, is he built like a Ken doll? He must be clean as a whistle on his sexual history to ironically have the balls to get all these women to talk to him about their sexual encounters.

Of course, there's the controversy over the sexual history that led to his birth. He's supposedly the offspring of Mia Farrow and Woody Allen, but it's often speculated by anyone with two eyes that he's really the son of "Old Blue Eyes," Frank Sinatra. It's not even that he looks like Frank, which he does; it's that he looks *nothing* like Woody Allen. You'd think a couple of recessive genes would make it into the mix, but apparently not. When Billy Joel's genes got together with Christie Brinkley's, they created a daughter who looked like both of them. When you breed a ten and a two, you end up with a six. Like when a poodle and a Labrador get together, the result is a Labradoodle. In Ronan Farrow's case, it would be like a poodle and a black Lab getting together and the puppy ending up a blonde Lab.

Just to close it out, which of Ronan's probable dads do you think is least proud of his work calling out guys with sketchy sexual pasts?

### Les Moonves

Again, I'm not surprised that a guy with the testosterone to drive him to the top of a major media corporation also wants to be on top of some of the women in that corporation. My real fury is about his wife, Julie Chen, who left *The Talk* after all the allegations against her man came out. What happened to the open, honest dialogue she'd been having with the other yentas on that show? She even left the show via a pretaped message, saying she was going to spend more time with Les. She's the female Matt Lauer. On a program that promotes itself as keeping it real, she was a real zero. No opinions, no comedic chops. She was right down the middle. She should totally give Les a pass, because he gave her a career. What are the chances that someone who had her personality surgically removed at birth would end up hosting not one but *two* network shows? Think about it. Has anyone ever uttered the phrase "Hey, did you hear what Julie Chen said the other day?"

But seriously, fuck Les Moonves. He didn't pick up my sitcom pilot for CBS in 2009 because, I was told, he liked blondes. Jenna Elfman had a pilot the same season, and he decided with his boner instead of his funny bone. I'm glad he got denied his $120 million golden parachute, like I got denied my pilot pickup.

## Jared Fogle

This one isn't so much a Me Too situation, but since we're covering the guys who actually deserved to lose their careers, I thought I'd throw him in. He's a real creep. And he's gonna be away for a long time. He's definitely going to put back on all the weight he lost eating Subway sandwiches. They'll be taking him out of that jail on a refrigerator dolly.

I do have a couple of ideas for him post-incarceration that would definitely make the news. If I were the CEO of Quiznos, I'd be locking down Jared as my spokesman right now. You can't buy that publicity. There's precedent from when the Verizon "Can you hear me now?" guy went to Sprint. Think of the balls it would take to hire Jared. It'd be like the "With a name like Smucker's, it has to be good" campaign. I'd stand at the front of the boardroom and say, "Hear me out. This move says we're so confident in our subs, we can have a convicted pedophile as our spokesman. We'll get more eyeballs than Ford, Coca-Cola, and Apple and never spend a nickel on marketing. It'll just be a picture of Jared holding one of our toasted subs with this line: "Quiznos: Yeah, we're that good!"

## Bill Cosby

Over the past few years, we've all seen the parade of women coming forward about getting drugged and raped by Bill Cosby. At a certain point, it would have been easier to just ask the female population of the United States between twenty-nine and sixty-four, "Who hasn't been roofied by 'the Cos'?"

I loved how in the wake of all these accusations, his honorary doctorates were all taken away. There you go. That'll solve the problem. "The fake degree we gave you to come and do our commencement speech is hereby revoked!" Why not take away something that stings? The certificates are still in the trunk of his car. I'm sure the honorary doctorate from Rutgers means as much to him as the certificate I have for finishing the Pig's Trough at Farrell's. ( Q Google It ) **bit.ly/ESA-Pig**

As I write this, he is in year one of a three- to ten-year sentence for aggravated indecent assault and is trying to appeal. Has anyone fallen from grace further than Bill Cosby? Some falls might have been faster, but this was America's dad, the voice of Jell-O and New Coke. The only question remaining is, does he kill himself in prison or does he die of...wait for it...natural Cos's? (Good stuff, Ace Man.) Seriously, if he were Japanese, he would have killed himself by now. Guys like this have such a high narcissism level that they see themselves as too good to die. Depressed sixteen-year-old boys kill themselves when their girlfriends break up with them. Harvey Weinstein, O. J. Simpson, Bill Clinton, and Bill Cosby are fine with themselves. Bill Cosby was narcissistic enough to sue his accusers. He made himself the victim. People like him don't look in the mirror and see monsters. Killing themselves would be denying the world their greatness.

I'll never be able to understand that mindset. What I really want to get to the bottom of is the women who stand by their men, or at least stand behind them tight-lipped and dead-eyed during their men's apologetic press conferences. I hope after Bill dies in prison, I can convince Camille Cosby to come with me. She'll still have some of his money left, and she'll defend every bad decision I ever make. She obviously knew about his transgressions and turned a blind eye. Seriously, if I were doing the deposition of Camille Cosby, my first question would have nothing to do with what she knew about his crimes; it'd be whether she has a younger sister with the same live-and-let-fuck attitude. I would then invite Camille to a dinner party with Lynette, Melania

Trump, and Anthony Weiner's wife, Huma Abedin. Eventually Lynette will start complaining about me and say, "The other day he came home, didn't say hi to the kids, and just went straight to the den." They'd each chime in. "Mine fucked a porn star at a golf tournament and then paid *The National Enquirer* to shut her up." "Mine sent a dick pic under the name Carlos Danger, taken while our infant son was in the bed with him." "Mine drugged and raped Playmates of the Year from 1972 through 2004, a quarter of the WNBA, and don't finish that drink. What were you saying about Adam being a little moody?"

Since the times we find ourselves in demand that people declare themselves a victim, I have a suggestion for all the above perpetrators. Rather than go into hiding, push back and claim that you are a *survivor* of a disorder that afflicts over three billion men worldwide: RCS, better known to the medical community as Restless Cock Syndrome. We can stop RCS in our lifetime. I'm wearing my white ribbon right now.

## The Collateral Damage

### Al Franken

I'm not defending Al because I like his politics or his comedy. I'm defending him because if there were a Mount Rushmore of guys who got fucked over in the rush to more judgment in the Me Too movement, he'd be George Washington (thus making him our first Jewish president). You've all seen the picture of him on the USO plane with Leeann Tweeden, his hands hovering over her flak jacket–covered chest while she is sleeping. It was clearly a joke. The stuff about his writing a scene specifically so she'd be forced to kiss him was debunked. But who cares? Those are just facts.

> (BTW) Trust me, you should never fall asleep in front of comedians. They are going to do horrible shit to you. My guest booker and road manager, Mike August, fell asleep during football-watching on Sunday, and Cousin Sal from *Jimmy Kimmel Live!* did a "Yokozuna" on him, jumping and landing with his bare ass on Mike's face. Mike reacted at the last second and ended up trying to block it, and chipped his tooth on his Rolex. And if you ever fall asleep in front of Jimmy Kimmel, you're definitely going to get a penis on your forehead. Hopefully, it will just be drawn in Sharpie. 😁

Al's plight did give me a great idea for a TV show, *Bus Bench with Al Franken*. Each week Al would sit on a bus bench like Forrest Gump and a different celebrity who has been "canceled" would sidle up next to him to talk about what they each did to lose their celebrity status. The premiere episode would have R. Kelly. Kelly would start: "I essentially kidnapped, brainwashed, and ritualistically raped a Girl Scout troop. It was pretty much my own personal sex cult. You?"

### Robert Kraft

Far be it from me as a Rams fan to want to help out anyone associated with the Patriots franchise, but this is another case of "We've got to make an example" bullshit. Yes, we've got to put an end to the scourge—nay, epidemic—of rich old widowers' getting HJs at Florida strip mall massage parlors. But because Robert Kraft was going to make the news, the police had to have a press conference, threaten to release the video evidence, and throw the book at the guy. I'm sure there are a couple thousand dudes in Florida who did the same thing but, ironically, got off clean because, like their balls post-massage, they were empty bags. Just because Kraft owns the Patriots and probably pays fifteen million dollars a year in taxes doesn't mean you get to make an example out of him. Just give him the same fine as the other dude from Orlando who spooged in the next room.

Police made a big deal out of having video evidence, which was bad news for Kraft's defense. When every article of clothing you wear is monogramed, you're going to be easily identified on a surveillance tape. It would have been great if they had sat him down, showed him the tape, and then brought Bill Belichick in to "break down the game film" and critique his handjob-receiving skills.

Speaking of hands, how quickly do the hands shoot up at the station house when the sergeant is looking for guys to go undercover to install the cameras and pretend to be businessmen getting happy endings at the rub-and-tug joint? I'm pretty sure there're a lot more volunteers for that duty than kicking down doors in the warehouse district to bust a drug ring. Not a tough call to choose between an MS-13 kid unloading a clip on you and a ninety-pound Asian broad unloading your clip for you.

I'm not justifying it, but as far as the accusation that Kraft was participating in, or at least benefiting from, "sex slavery," there are worse options as far as slavery goes. I'm not a historian, but when I think about the Jews in Egypt, or Africans in the South, I imagine any one of them would rather give Kraft a handy than be sweating in the fields getting whipped picking cotton or in a pit making bricks from mud and straw.

Before we move on, let's talk about the rub and tug. First off, no one could ever give as good a handjob as you can give yourself, so this act has no appeal to me. More important, I would prefer a tug and rub rather than a rub and tug. If you do the tugging first, then I can enjoy the rub during my refractory period. If I get the massage first, I'm going to be anxious about when the tugging is going to start.

Another quick Robert Kraft story related to our commander in chief. I was backstage at the finale of *The Celebrity Apprentice* in the little green room area they had created out of draped black Duvetyne. (To all the aspiring female black rappers or ebony porn stars reading this, Duvetyne would make a great name. You're welcome.) I was hanging out with the male celebrities having some drinks and snacks when Trump walked in and said, "Guys, I'm going to get Bob Kraft and introduce him to you all." You could tell he was proud, like he was going to blow our minds. He didn't know the crew he was pitching this experience to. It was Paul Senior from Orange County Choppers—he's a biker, so he's not into team sports; Dee Snider from Twisted Sister—he's a rock-and-roll guy, so he's not into sports in general; Penn Jillette, the magic nerd; plus Clay Aiken and George Takei. Need I say more? What are the chances that six men are offered the chance to meet the rich owner of what will likely go down as the greatest franchise in NFL history, and none of them know who the fuck he is? I was the only one in the room who wasn't assuming Trump's friend Bob Kraft was the heir to the macaroni-and-cheese fortune.

## Peter Farrelly

I hope you're sitting down. The director of *There's Something About Mary*, *Dumb and Dumber*, and *Kingpin* goofed around on the set. Take a minute to catch your breath if you need to. In the run-up to winning the Oscar for *The Green Book*, he had to apologize for something he had done a decade before. Apparently, he liked to pull down his pants and expose himself to actors to make them laugh. You know who thought it was funny? Cameron Diaz.

It's all about context. This is friends fucking around on a movie set. Growing up, every guy I knew would pull a nut out of their fly and let it dangle until their friend noticed. God forbid you left your camera out at a party; you'd have the film developed and there'd be a picture of a graduating girl in her cap and gown, a custom cake done up like a soccer field, and your buddy Craig's cock and balls.

## Matt Damon

This one is particularly stupid, because Matt Damon didn't do anything. He simply pointed out that Al Franken didn't do anything. But in the Me Too witch hunt, pointing out context, gradations of offenses, and proportionate outrage apparently makes you a witch too. There was far more indignation about Matt Damon's pointing out that there is a difference between Al Franken and Harvey Weinstein than there was about the officer who stood outside Marjory Stoneman Douglas High School while seventeen kids got gunned down. The poor guy took so much shit, he can't even get booked on Kimmel.

## James Franco

I'm not even really sure what he did other than be young and hot in Hollywood and mow his way through starlets. He won a Golden Globe for *The Disaster Artist* and was likely to get an Oscar nod, but then he put on a Me Too support lapel pin and made himself a target. He was trying to show his support, but that only made the mob go after him.

On this one I say, "Good, douche. You got what was coming to you." The part where he's a human and had transgressions I'm okay with; that's up to him and the people he wronged to sort out. The part where he had to climb to the top of Mount Pious and declare himself a hero only to get outed as a poon-hound is just good karma.

### William Shatner

Who would have thought that Captain Kirk would turn out to be Captain Creep? Mr. Spock would find his sexual harassment highly illogical.

I bet half of you right now are thinking, "I didn't even hear about that one," but you believed it for a second. That's the problem with this movement. For a split second I made you think Shatner committed some offense beyond his hairpiece when he hasn't. But in this fucked-up time, rumor weighs as much as fact, and once someone gets that scarlet hashtag, it's hard to shake. There were plenty of guys who did nothing wrong, like my friends Chris Hardwick and Neil deGrasse Tyson, two of the nicest, nerdiest guys on the planet who wouldn't hurt a fly, never mind a girlfriend or an intern, who got caught in the accusation-equals-guilt thresher and forever will be a footnote in the history, or should I say hysteria, of the Me Too moment.

### Charlie Rose and Garrison Keillor

In case you were wondering, I didn't forget about them. I'm not sure of the details of what Charlie Rose did or if Garrison Keillor did anything at all. What I do know is that if Charlie Rose, the PBS host, and Garrison Keillor, the soft-spoken voice from Lake Wobegon, can get Me Too'd, then it's possible for any of us. There's no more "That guy would never...." Think about it. They faced the same public shaming and scrutiny that Donald Trump and Harvey Weinstein did. That is the full range of male sexuality. Every one of us males falls between those two goalposts.

## *Richard Ned Lebow*

Don't know that name, do you? By the end of this section, you'll understand why you should. He was a professor of political theory at King's College London. Here's another name you don't know: Simona Sharoni, a professor of women's and gender studies at Merrimack College in Massachusetts.

The long story short is that they were at a convention of scholars who study international affairs. Among many others, they were jammed in an elevator. I'm sure at this point you're thinking that he grabbed her tit, squeezed her ass cheek, or rubbed himself up against her. If only. Everyone was yelling out their floor, and the seventy-six-year-old Lebow made the dumb old "Fifth floor, women's lingerie" joke. Well, apparently this bitch Professor Sharoni did not hear a tired joke from a Bugs Bunny cartoon; she heard a vicious attack and demanded an apology. She filed a formal complaint with the International Studies Association (ISA). After Professor Lebow's first round of reaching out to her to humbly explain the joke was rejected, and the ISA required him to cease contact with her, he wrote the following to her.

> *Like you, I am strongly opposed to the exploitation, coercion, or humiliation of women. As such evils continue, it seems to me to make sense to direct our attention to real offenses, not those that are imagined or marginal. By making a complaint to ISA that I consider frivolous—and I expect, will be judged this way by the ethics committee—you may be directing time and effort away from the real offenses that trouble us both.*

She took offense that he called her frivolous offense frivolous, and the ISA told him to formally apologize. This hero refused. He must have read the preface of this book two years before it was written. I'm sure there are many who are reading this and thinking he should have just capitulated and moved on. But he is right. Giving in would only encourage more of this over-reactive bullshit, which prevents action on real problems. This would be like a new police chief saying he's going to be tough on crime and clean up the city, and his first act is hitting jaywalkers with pepper spray while the Latin Kings are filling the streets with fentanyl.

When you become a professor of women's and gender studies, don't you just become like a pig finding truffles, tuning your sniffer to hunt down every potential offense toward women? Of course Professor Sharoni found something to complain about. She tipped her hand in her original complaint when she wrote, "As a survivor of sexual harassment in the academy, I am quite shaken by this incident." To make things worse, she highlighted that the people on the elevator were "all white middle-aged men, except for myself and another woman." Why the need to include his race or the race of the other people in the elevator who laughed if you're not looking to make yourself into a victim of the current boogeyman for all of society's ills, the middle-aged white guy? If everyone in the elevator laughed except you, maybe you're the fucking problem. Do us all a favor: take the elevator to the roof and jump off.

One last quick idea. I think I'm going to do a spin-off with Professor Lebow much like *Bus Bench with Al Franken*. I'll put him in an elevator with a special celebrity guest to discuss their elevator behavior and consequences—Ray Rice. ( Google It )
**bit.ly/ESA-Rice**

Our next and final entrant is not white but did fall victim to someone seeking to be a victim.

### Aziz Ansari

Like many, I'm not sure what he did other than go on a bad date. All I know is that he shouldn't have apologized. He should have held a press conference, come out, and said, "I'm Aziz and I Ain't Sari," before dropping the mic and walking off.

This is the problem. The rules of the game have changed. We're all capable of offending in the current culture. I would hate to be dating now. I'd be horrible at online dating. I'd start looking for someone to have a date with, jump over to YouJizz, deplete myself, and then the girl I was chatting with on the dating site would be like, "You want to go to California Pizza Kitchen?" "Nah, I'm good. I'm just going to watch *SportsCenter*." Actually, I'd probably have the girl describe herself, punch that into the search on Pornhub, and just take care of myself.

I can't type worth a shit either. I'd need some sort of Cybero de Bergerac to make sure I didn't screw up my profile. Otherwise I'd be one wrong keystroke away from writing about all the millions I spend collecting vintage rape cars.

All the dating app stuff has ruined the cute stories we heard about our parents and grandparents courting each other. It used to be: "I had a friend who needed to set up his girlfriend's friend so he could go on a double date. So he asked me and I didn't want to go, but I owed him a favor. At first it didn't go well. Your mother didn't think I was interested, because it was a setup. But I knew that there was something special about her. So I was persistent. I kept asking for a date with just the two of us until she finally gave in and I won her over. I put that florist's kid through college sending your mother a bouquet a day until she agreed." My grandkids are going to ask their parents how they met, and the answer will simply be: "Dad swiped right." And that persistence part would be called stalking today.

I'd never send a dick pic. It seems like it's standard protocol nowadays to send a snapshot of your dong to the gal you're courting. Imagine if this was always the case, if part of dating was snapping a Polaroid of your pecker, stuffing it in an envelope, and mailing it to your potential gal pal. I'll never understand this, but I guess that says something about my cock. I don't feel the need to show it off. It's not big, there's no novelty to it, it doesn't dogleg in an interesting way or have a birthmark the shape of Idaho. It's not like some dicks that are veiny and look like Wolverine's neck. It's just a standard issue white-guy dick. There's no need for a picture of my dick. If you want to know what it looks like, next time you're making s'mores, stack up three marshmallows. It'd be like if you and your buddy were walking down the street and he stopped you and said, "Hold up, hold up...is that a Camry? Dude, that's an '05 beige Camry with a cloth interior. Get a picture!" If my dick were a character from a sitcom, it would be Potsie from *Happy Days*. ( Google It ) **bit.ly/ESA-Potsie2** Nothing to write home about or spin off into its own series.

## Statutory Rock

Another victim of the Me Too movement is Frank Loesser, songwriter of "Baby, It's Cold Outside." There was a lot of hubbub about this Christmas tune in 2018 with some radio stations refusing to play it. While the line "Say, what's in this drink?" does evoke Cosbyesque imagery, it's hardly the rapiest tune out there that's still on the airwaves. Hear Casey Kasem in your head as we count down the top ten "statutory rock" tunes of all time.

Coming in at number ten is a hot track from Neil Diamond, which is a given to make our "Too Young to Consent" countdown: "Girl, You'll Be a Woman Soon."

*Girl, you'll be a woman soon. Please, come take my hand*
*Girl, you'll be a woman soon. Soon, you'll need a man*

Incidentally, there's a deeper cut by Neil Diamond with a line that pegs the creep-o-meter: "September Morn."

*Look at what you've done. Why, you've become a grown-up girl*
*I still can hear you crying, in a corner of your room.*

Why is she crying, Neil? What did you do?!

Coming in at number nine, which is half the age these girls should be, is "Christine Sixteen" by KISS.

*I don't usually say things like this to girls your age, but when I*
*saw you coming out of school that day, that day I knew, I knew, I've*
*got to have you!*

Disgusting, but still Shakespeare compared to the lyrics of "Lick It Up!"

Coming in at number eight on the countdown is Sammy Johns's 1973 ode to mobile rape wagons, "Chevy Van."

*Her young face was like that of an angel*
*Her long legs were tanned and brown*

Yes, Sammy picks up a young hitchhiker who is "like a princess," "makes love" to her in his Chevy Van and then "puts her out" in a small town in her bare feet and never passes through again. Yes, Sammy, you were truly the Prince Charming to that princess.

Number seven on our countdown wastes no time in letting you know a crime is about to be committed. Here are the opening lyrics of Benny Mardones's number-eleven Hot 100 hit in 1980, "Into the Night."

*She's just sixteen years old*
*Leave her alone, they say*

If by "they" he means her parents, the police, her high school guidance counselor, and society in general, then yes, "they" say to leave her alone. Since this was Benny's only hit, it makes me wonder whether when he's playing the county fair circuit and has to close with this tune, he changes the lyrics. "She's well over eighteen years old..." Or maybe he modifies it based on each state's age of consent. When he's playing the Alabama State Fair, he wouldn't need to change a thing.

Number six on the countdown has the word "child" right in the title. From 1978, Nick Gilder's "Hot Child in the City."

*So young to be loose and on her own*
*Young boys they all want to take her home*

I don't know which city this is, but I hope they have a good Megan's Law sex offender registry map if I ever move there.

Starting out the top half of our rape-rock wrap-up is a perennial all-star with multiple entries. Number five is Gary Puckett & the Union Gap's "Lady Willpower." Starting as a typical 1968 love song, it later gives us a window into the object of Gary's desire with this set of lyrics.

*Did no one ever tell you the facts of life?*
*Well there's so much you have to learn.*

Just in case that didn't let you know that the lyricists liked them barely pubescent, number four on our list is also by Gary Puckett, and lays it out in the title of the song: "Young Girl." It's hard to pick just which lyric is the creepiest. Look them up for yourself and decide, but I'm going with:

*Beneath your perfume and make-up*
*You're just a baby in disguise*

While a lot of songs use the word "baby" figuratively, this one uses it literally.

Number three on our countdown tells the story of how a man everyone called "yellow" finally finds his courage after his love, "Becky," is raped. From 1979, "Coward of the County," sung by Kenny Rogers.

*One day while he was working, the Gatlin boys came calling*
*They took turns at Becky, and there was three of them.*

Nothing like a little gang rape in the middle of your peppy country song. Fun fact: They were named the Gatlin boys in the song because the songwriter allegedly had a grudge against country stars The Gatlin Brothers, of which there were actually three.

On to number two in our countdown. While the 1970s were the heyday for retro rape rock, 1988 brought us Winger's "Seventeen."

*She's only seventeen. Daddy says she's too young,*
*but she's old enough for me.*

You won't find that song on *Best of Winger*. Because there is no *Best of Winger*.

And claiming the number one spot on the chart, with their third and strongest entry, Gary Puckett & the Union Gap from 1969 with "This Girl Is a Woman Now."

*She cried a single tear, a teardrop that was sweet and warm*
*...A child had died, a woman had been born*

While in the lyrics of "Young Girl," the songwriter tells her to "get out of my mind" because their love is "way out of line," the protagonist of "This Girl Is a Woman Now" clearly followed through on his temptations. Google the rest of the lyrics, which talk about "a child existing in a playground of stone," who is "learning how to give," then take a shower and come back to finish this chapter.

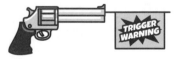

If you find yourself on the following list, prepare to be triggered. Somewhere in 2017 it hit me that Natalie Portman would be disgusted to have sex with me. From there it grew to a top-thirty list that my podcast fans nominate and rank annually of female celebrities who would find not only my body but my soul disgusting. I'm sure none of them will read this chapter, but if they do they will only be more horrified if, somehow, we end up having sex. Again, to be clear, while there may be some crossover, this isn't a list of notable women I want to have sex with. My nonexistent self-esteem wouldn't let me make such a list. A blue-ribbon panel I commissioned has combined the rankings from 2017, 2018, and 2019, eliminated the inside jokes and family members that fans put on the list to fuck with me, and created the definitive, all-star, hall-of-fame list of women who would never stop vomiting if they had sex with me.

This is the one who started it all. She played Jackie Kennedy, but she'd be more traumatized than the actual Jackie Kennedy if she had to hump me. She'd pour Dior perfume into her eyes—*Natalie Portman.*

I called her a crazy cooze and told her to go back to South Africa for her comments about America being racist. For her, a little afternoon delight with me would be equivalent to the postapocalyptic hell of *Mad Max: Fury Road*—*Charlize Theron.*

The screams of terror and disgust she'd make having sex with me might actually be an improvement on her "music." Doing it with me would be more horrifying for her than that fateful night at the Dakota—*Yoko Ono.*

As a gay man, he technically qualifies for the list. He's stood in hurricanes, seen the horrors of war up close, but nothing would break this breaker of breaking news like a good rodgering from the Ace Man. I'm not sure if he's a top or a bottom, but I'm sure he'd rather be at the bottom of a lake than have sex with me—*Anderson Cooper.*

She's the media mogul who would be so ruined for sex after getting with me that she'd have even *less* sex with Stedman. Getting nailed by me would not be living her best fearless life in the now and would definitely not be one of her favorite things—*Oprah Winfrey*.

The liberals should pray I never bang my gavel in this judge, because I'd break her brittle elderly bones and give Trump another Supreme Court nomination. This member of SCOTUS wouldn't want to see my scrotus—*Ruth Bader Ginsburg*.

The list wouldn't be complete without this MVP (most vomiting person). This host of *The View* would rather view an oncoming train than me coming—*Joy Behar*.

We both love racing and share some of the same political views. But after sex with me, she'd have trouble finding a bathroom in North Carolina in which to vomit—*Caitlyn Jenner*.

She'd hate having sex with me as much as she hates corporate greed and the uneven playing field. After humping me, her spirit would be Broke-a-hontas—*Elizabeth Warren*.

She made the list all three years. We might even agree on politics, but she's probably still mad at me for hanging up on her when she called in late to my radio show in 2006. On the bright side, if I was inside her, for a change she'd be filled with something other than hate—*Ann Coulter*.

Also, a perennial on the list, she hates everything I stand for, and she could do a long editorial on MSNBC about how disgusted she was—*Rachel Maddow*.

She'd end her lifestyle blog and probably just end her life. She wouldn't want any of my goop—*Gwyneth Paltrow*.

She wasn't on the list in 2017, because we didn't know who the fuck she is. But even though she hates guns, she was number one with a bullet in 2018. Hispanic, Democratic, young, and attractive, she would be horrified. She'd go from "AOC" to RIP—*Alexandria Ocasio-Cortez.*

She hates me because she thinks I said women aren't funny (even though I never did). But she makes me think what I didn't say *is* true. She starred in *Girls,* and she'd probably have sex only with girls after doing the deed with me—*Lena Dunham.*

And last but not least, 2019's winner. She'd weep openly with her daughter and then podcast about it—*Alyssa Milano.*

In closing, it seems like the Me Too fever has broken a little bit, but I'm sure there are more guys who are going to get taken out—some who deserve it and some who don't. The good news is, I used to be ashamed of masturbating alone, but in the post–Harvey Weinstein and Louis C. K. world, I'm a hero. I have the class, dignity, and social justice bona fides to beat the bejesus out of my cock behind closed doors without any witnesses. In a word, I'm brave.

# Chapter 8

# From Primates to Postmates: The De-evolution of a Species

I've spent the previous seven chapters breaking down how we've broken down as a society. I looked a lot at where we are now and how we got here. Now, let me put the Adam in Nostradamus and look a little into the future to see where we're heading. It ain't pretty, but there's still a chance for us to do something about it.

## Wired for Weakness

We are at a weird point in our evolutionary history. Up until the past few hundred years, which is a blink when it comes to evolution, we did not toy with any notion of self-government. We were governed by nature. We planted in the spring and harvested in the fall. We killed a buffalo in the summer and made sure it lasted through the winter, or we would die. We did not need self-control. Nature did that for us. But we have an internal mechanism that says, "I don't want to chase a wildebeest around for three days and hope to kill it." It's called the law of conservation of energy. It's why cats sleep all day and bears hibernate. It's our biology to expend as little energy as possible. The nature of humans is to want to crawl back up our mom's pussy and take a nap. It used to be that if we didn't expend enough energy to hunt, chop wood for winter, and carry water from the well, we'd die. We're in a very dangerous place now where we're getting our wishes. That same law of conservation of energy gave us butchers and super-markets. After that we no longer needed to hunt and prepare the meat. Someone did it for us. Technology has now made it possible for us to no longer need to pick it up or cook it either. In the past, the entire world was tilted against our getting fat. We spent more calories getting food than we got from it. It's the exact opposite now. Now there's Panda Express at nine a.m. for four dollars.

Last New Year's, I made the declaration to my wife and kids that we would only eat the leftovers from the Christmas and New Year's parties, to be less wasteful. We had a fridge full of good stuff—brisket and Chinese food. After making my family's reso-lution for them, I took a nap. Forty-five minutes later, I woke up to find Subway *and* McDonald's on my kitchen counter. I'll save the rant on the passive-aggressive part of that and focus on the convenience.

At first I was confused by this Grubhub, DoorDash, and Post-mates shit. One day I was leaving the house at nine in the morning and saw a heavyset nineteen-year-old gal walking toward me up my driveway. I didn't know what to make of it. She was too old to be selling Girl Scout cookies, too young to be hawking Avon or Mary Kay, and not dressed well enough to be a Jehovah's Wit-ness. Then I noticed what she was carrying. I thought, *Who is this person, and why is she carrying a Carl's Jr. bag?* Did she have the wrong address? Was this some crazed fan out to stab me like

George Harrison? Eventually she got to me and handed me the bag, wordlessly. I was thinking, *Why did this traveling saleswoman just hand me her breakfast?* She read the look on my face and said simply, "Grubhub." It turns out Natalia had ordered breakfast chicken bites, which I didn't even know existed, never mind that they were an item that a portly teen could schlep to your door.

In retrospect, I think it started with Taco Bell delivery. I wrote *Not Taco Bell Material*, but I have a lot of Taco Bell material. They will not rest until our livers explode. First, they invented the fourth meal, then they got a soft taco to rape a hard-shell taco and called it a gordita, then they covered all the tacos in Dorito dust, and finally they started driving it to your house. You can't drive or walk one block to Taco Bell? And nothing is a better value, weight-wise. You spend $4.85 and you'll hyperextend your elbow carrying it out.

I think Mexico has been trying to reclaim the Southwest through ranchera music, blaring that horrible crap so we'll all eventually just say, "Fuck it, I'm moving to Connecticut. My kid has to study for an algebra final, and all I can hear is tuba and accordion." Now I'm thinking Taco Bell is in on it, fattening us up so we can't fight back. They will not rest until we do nothing but rest.

Then there was the time I went out with Lynette for our sixteenth anniversary. We left Natalia and Sonny by themselves. Olga the nanny was out of town. God forbid they make themselves a meal, so we allowed them to have some friends over and order from Postmates.

I came home to find a large cheese pizza with two slices taken out, but the cheese from those two slices was piled on the side of the cardboard box. I immediately started thinking of ways to bring the pizza into the office and force my employees to eat it.

Unlike my kids and their friends, I can't let that go to waste. I'm now at the point where I'm considering getting a pig in the back of the house. There's so much wasted food at my abode, I just need a slop trough and a hog to eat this shit.

( BTW ) It occurred to me recently that bad pizza smells better than good pizza. It tastes like cardboard and has the texture of Nerf, but the thick, doughy garbage from the concession stand at the auto show or the ballpark, even the rectangular pizza from school that tastes like a yoga mat covered in Ragu, smells better than the good thin-crust New York style. I guess it's over-compensation. 😬

After my pizza-cheese outrage subsided, I found myself in Sonny's room, where I noticed a bag from Shake Shack. The kids had ordered from two different places! Two different delivery people had darkened my doorstep with two different orders from two different restaurants. When I was growing up, if you had suggested to my father that we could go out to two different restaurants in one night, never mind having two different restaurants deliver, he would react the same as if you waved a log on fire in front of a Cro-Magnon man. He would have just grunted in fear and confusion.

On that note, I was driving around L.A. recently and saw a sign at Jack in the Box, which, for those of you not in the region, is a poorer man's McDonald's. It read, "We Accept EBT." If you don't know what that stands for, congratulations, winner. It's electronic benefit transfer, formerly known as food stamps. I know I'm the angry rich guy, but it's fucking infuriating that our government allows tax money to be put on a card so poor people can kill themselves with shitty food. In my opinion, if that ain't your money, you shouldn't get that crap. I want you eating good meat, eggs, cheese, and produce. Who's paying for the diabetes you're getting from this culinary abortion? As a former food-stamp kid who grew up on welfare, desperate for a decent meal, I am driven insane by this.

We have lost the sense of food's value in this culture. But not all of us. I recently saw Olga the nanny pulling every piece of gristle, tendon, and fat off the chicken bones from one of our dinners and putting it in a Ziploc bag for Phil. She gets the value of food. The Native Americans used every piece of the buffalo because Grubhub didn't exist. There was no FlapDash dropping a bison off at their teepees. They had to go on a hundred-mile three-day odyssey from which some of them didn't return in order to get that buffalo, so they were going to use every fucking part of it. It's like the Kardashians; they film every part of their lives and turn it into something. My kids don't eat every part of their burger from Shake Shack because a loser delivered it, so it has no value.

I'm not immune to this. I have a steam shower in my house. It's all tile. Well, I don't want to sit on ninety-degree tile, because that would be like sitting on a curb in summer. I was looking for something better than just a folded towel, something that could take the heat and damp without falling apart. So, I made my assistant look for it for weeks. It was a two-month saga of follow-ups with Matt trying to find the right steam-shower ass coaster. One day I just said, "Type in 'steam room pillow' and see what comes up." He found one that was antimicrobial, had adequate cushioning for the Ace Man's ass, and looked good. We ordered it, and I waited anxiously. I followed up a couple days later to get a status update. Matt told me, "Amazon is going to deliver it today." I was very excited about my steam-room butt pillow. All day I kept looking at the front door, pacing feverishly, ready to put it to use. I was like a kid on Christmas, except that kid was Jewish and there were no gifts coming. No package was delivered. I announced to the heavens that this was a disaster and, of course, this is what happens to me. Could it go any other way?

As I was heading out to do stand-up, dejected, the Amazon guy pulled up, walked about fifteen feet up the driveway, and dropped the package. I was outraged. I had been fantasizing all day about sitting on the pillow in my steam room, but this asshole delivered it late, right as I was driving away, so I had to wait until the next day for my asshole to enjoy it. *Bullshit!*

It then hit me that I hadn't ordered it from Amazon. I had told my assistant to order it from Amazon. I hadn't even overcome the lethargy to google it myself and enter my credit-card number; I'd had Matt do it. And I was angry that the delivery guy hadn't walked it to the front door of my seven-million-dollar house with a steeply graded driveway. Did this jagoff expect me to walk fifteen feet, on my own property, *downhill?!!!!*

This wasn't medication for my diabetic infant. This was so my rich white ass didn't have to sit on a towel. This is fall-of-the-Roman-Empire shit. Add in the copious amounts of pornography I consume, and I'm an ostrich feather fan and a virgin feeding me peeled grapes away from going full Caligula.

The other day, I had a sad realization about how lazy we've gotten when I was talking to Lynette about our Roomba robot vacuum. I noticed it was not being used and asked her why. She said because you have to charge it in its little doghouse and clean out the dustbin once a month. I said, "Are you telling me we're too lazy to own a robot?"

We're going to convenience ourselves out of existence. We need to rein this in quickly before we end up like the fat-asses hovering around in chairs in *Wall-E*. The ball has been snapped, and the play is on. We have to do this on the fly. Eventually we'll be calling Lyft to say, "Send over a drone. I'm on the toilet, and I really need to get to the sofa."

## Master of the You-Niverse

There's only one way out of this, and it's not going to be something we can buy and have delivered. It comes from within. We are going to need to learn to master ourselves. Now, I had a head start on learning to deprive myself and subjecting my body to extremes. As readers of *Not Taco Bell Material* know, I lived in an uninsulated service porch that "identified" as my room. When I lived in my dad's A-frame house, I was at the top of that A in an unventilated attic doing Bikram yoga before it was trendy. The only thing emptier than that attic was our fridge.

With convenience being so convenient nowadays, we are going to have to force ourselves into circumstances that mirror those of our caveman ancestors—which, if you judge by the hair on my ass, was probably only two generations ago.

One of the simplest-to-understand but hardest-to-achieve ways of challenging yourself is NSNG—"No Sugar, No Grain," for the uninitiated. I'm not going to get into the weeds on NSNG. This isn't a celebrity diet book; there are plenty of those on the market. You can google my friend and frequent podcast guest Vinnie Tortorich to find out all about it, but the title should be self-explanatory. Turns out that while we were being fed stuff that was killing us, we were also being fed a line of bullshit. That line goes all the way back to the founding of the Kellogg company, progressed all the way through the SnackWell's era of the '80s and the USDA food pyramid in 1992, and is going strong today with the Impossible Burger craze—it says that grain is good and meat is murder. Grains and bread are literally the foundation of the U.S. government's food pyramid, meat is the second-smallest section near the top, and fats are at the pinnacle, along with "sweets." Fat makes for a perfect enemy. It has the word "fat" right in the name. "Fat will make you fat." Turns out, that idea is as true as the old notion that being out in the cold will give you a cold. The government has the food pyramid completely upside down, much like many other bullshit ideas hatched by the government and forced down the throat of every schoolkid. I know hundreds of people who have rapidly lost weight and increased energy, including myself, doing NSNG. That's the side benefit. But my point is larger than that. Sugar is addictive, and it's hard to break that habit. And that's why it's important. The real win with NSNG is that you are fighting that inner child who is hooked on Sugar Smacks. You're facing your infantile cravings and punishing yourself a little to achieve greater health. We need to get away from what I call the Yummy Phase. We all know the people who are stuck in a child-like mentality and would eat macaroni and cheese for every meal. Maybe you're one of them. Take this quick test to see if you're stuck in the Yummy Phase:

## Yummy Phase Test

Pick one from each category below and check the box.

### Starbucks Order

1. Black coffee ☐
2. Coffee with cream ☐
3. Coffee with cream and sugar ☐
4. Flavored coffee (vanilla, hazelnut, mocha, etc.) ☐
5. Some blended Frappuccino thing with whipped cream and a dome lid ☐

### Alcoholic Drink

1. Gin martini ☐
2. Scotch on the rocks ☐
3. Beer or red wine ☐
4. White wine ☐
5. Daiquiri, piña colada, or other blended fruity drink ☐

### Steak

1. Rare ☐
2. Medium rare ☐
3. Medium ☐
4. Well done ☐
5. Well done with ketchup ☐

### Side Dish

1. Asparagus ☐
2. Creamed spinach ☐
3. Baked potato ☐
4. Mashed potatoes ☐
5. Macaroni and cheese ☐

## Seafood

**1.** Sashimi ☐
**2.** Broiled salmon ☐
**3.** Shrimp cocktail ☐
**4.** Breaded calamari ☐
**5.** Fish and chips ☐

## After the Meal

**1.** Cigar ☐
**2.** Brandy ☐
**3.** Cheese plate ☐
**4.** Pie ☐
**5.** Cake and ice cream ☐

## Sports

**1.** UFC ☐
**2.** Boxing ☐
**3.** Football ☐
**4.** Baseball ☐
**5.** Soccer ☐

## Eating Pussy and/or Sucking Cock

**1.** I'm doing it now. ☐
**2.** Every time we make love. ☐
**3.** On our anniversary. ☐
**4.** Only when I'm really drunk. ☐
**5.** I'm going to vomit in my mouth. ☐

*(continued)*

Add the total of your chosen numbers.

**Total Yummy Phase score:** _____

## Scoring Guide

The higher the number, the "yummier" you are.

| | |
|---|---|
| **0–8** | You're my hero. |
| **9–16** | We could definitely hang out. |
| **17–24** | Congratulations, you're an adult. |
| **25–32** | You're a child. |
| **33–40** | You're a special needs child. |

The message translates beyond the taste buds. This is about learning to appreciate that which doesn't immediately give you pleasure. Why has the price of everything except food inflated? The price of your house has gone up, the price of your car has gone up, but a pizza or a taco from Taco Bell is still as cheap as it was when I got rejected from working there. Because it's trash full of sugar, artificial flavors, preservatives, and additives. But we keep going back to it, or rather, we keep having it delivered to our lazy, ever-widening asses. The corporations producing this slop know they have us hooked and are tapping into something primitive and immature: the need for immediate gratification and to avoid pain.

Punishing yourself a little is a good thing. And in today's society, it's fucking necessary. You need to murder your inner child. Perhaps you should drown it in a pool, like I did. Here's another example from my own life.

I live in the foothills of the San Gabriel Mountains in an area called La Cañada. It's a little bit like Mayberry; you wouldn't even know you were mere minutes from that homeless-filled hellhole known as Los Angeles. Being in the hills, it can get colder at night than other parts of Southern California. This is where the self-inflicted discomfort comes in. Four months of the year, that means my pool can get into the forty-to-fifty-degree range. For over three years, I have been dunking myself in that pool daily, often before dawn. Naked. It's stimulating. The number-one response people give me when I tell them to do this is, "But it's so cold. I don't want to do that." Exactly. The answer is in the answer. You don't *want* to do that. But you *should*. When you get out of that freezing pool, you are completely woke, and not bullshit Brooklyn hipster "woke." It stops you from sleepwalking around all morning in a bathrobe followed by an afternoon crash.

You'll tingle all day. You put yourself in harm's way intentionally and get the benefit of pushing past your comfort zone. If you have the means, I highly recommend it. If not, do what I do in the summer—take a nice icy-cold shower. I'll leave it to a scientist to tell you the health benefits of this. All I know is you'll never feel more alive.

I'm not into cleanses or fasting, but I appreciate those ideas. I don't buy the bullshit about "removing toxins"; but I love the part about putting yourself in check and punishing yourself, though everyone I've ever met who's on a cleanse is a douche. The first toxin that comes out of your ass in liquid form is apparently your sense of humor.

The key to all of this, whether it's NSNG, the cold-pool dunk, fasting, hot yoga, walking on hot coals, running a marathon, or doing a Tough Mudder, is that you have to inflict it on yourself. You don't feel like you got a good workout if you run from a bear. Leonardo DiCaprio's character in *The Revenant* didn't feel like he got a workout; he was just surviving. If you run through the woods without being chased, you get something out of it. It has to be chosen.

This is the next step in evolution, being able to control yourself. I don't care if my kids get college degrees, but if they can look at that piece of pecan pie and say nay, I've done my job. With that self-discipline, you can turn mountains into speed bumps, and then life is yours.

## Use Your Hands or Lose Your Mind

In movies we have apocalyptic visions of machines turning on us—*The Terminator, Maximum Overdrive, 2001: A Space Odyssey*. But in real life, it won't be a robot with a machine gun in its hand killing you; it will be the robot in your hand. We're not all emergency neurosurgeons. We don't need to be reachable at all times. It's narcissism and it's killing us.

Every Sunday when I was a lad, I'd see the neighborhood dads and their kids out in the sun washing their cars. It was common. I'd see the stream of water running down the street from where Mr. Johnson was up the block washing his Buick. I haven't seen that in a long time. I live in L.A., where everyone is a piece of shit, but I think this is common across the country. There used to be a quiet dignity in "I'll wash it myself" that we've lost. It takes time. You have to prepare the bucket and soapy water, get that sponge glove, give the car the once-over twice, and then hose it down.

Now, if you said you were going to wash your car, your friend would say, "Don't be a sucker. Take it to the corner and give a Mexican seven dollars to wash it. You don't have time. You can afford it." Yes, but you can't afford *not* to do it.

This mentality is especially killing males, because the disconnect from the tangible world and immersion in the virtual world has made them unable to apply logic. Adult men are struggling with reason, and I think technology is the problem. When every action is virtual, so are the consequences. Take my old field. Construction is a logic-and-reason puzzle. You need to do things sequentially, to measure twice and cut once, or there are consequences, potentially deadly ones. Guys who work on offshore oil derricks need to have more logic and reason than people who work in tech, because if the offshore guys fuck up, they'll get hit with a pipe and fall into the ocean. We need to do more with our physical bodies in order to challenge our brains. It used to be part of life. You needed to figure out how to dig a well or you wouldn't survive. We used to have mines; now we have Minecraft. We used to have farms; now we have FarmVille. We used to fight wars;

now we have World of Warcraft. We used to dodge actual barrels thrown by an ape; now we have Donkey Kong. (Okay, I took that one step too far.)

My point is that when we stopped chopping wood and carrying water, we invented the gym to make up the deficit. We stopped needing to row, so we invented rowing machines. We stopped walking and started driving, so we invented treadmills. We figured out pretty quickly on the physical end that we're going to need to burn some calories. We need to do the same thing with the other part of our bodies that is atrophying—our brains. You notice yourself getting fat, but you don't notice yourself getting dumb and discontented, irritable and unsatisfied. Lack of gratitude and the inability to delay gratification sneak up on you. Before you know it, you've got the society I've spent this book complaining about. We're going to need to make mental conditioning a part of our life's rituals, just as we've done with physical conditioning. The problem is, you can sell a Bowflex, a Peloton bike, or a SoulCycle class, but there's no industry for "take a hike through a forest while listening to Mozart." No one can sell you "go down to the beach and throw the Frisbee to your kid in the surf." And there's certainly no money to be made on things that are difficult. We're going to have to foist those upon ourselves.

I say we go full Amish. You know how the Amish have Rumspringa, when the teens get to drink, cavort, and generally do crazy shit, like using light switches? We need to have the opposite of this, when all of us who are stuck in a virtual world go and do some old-fashioned barn raising for a few weeks. You never saw anybody with a long beard named Hezekiah saying he had a bad back from churning butter, or whining on Yelp that his food took an extra five minutes to arrive because the horse pulling the carriage to deliver it threw a shoe.

## The Future of the Species—Homos and Sapiens

So, where are we headed? We always talk about the shrinking middle class. There's another class that is shrinking: average dudes. In the future, all we're going to have are superpuss and extreme dude. The "haves" and "have nots" will be those who have genitalia and those who don't. I believe strongly that mixed martial arts is the fastest-growing sport because we're all in air-conditioned cars and ergonomically designed chairs. This disconnection with the real, hard world that our forebears contended with is going to turn us into soft, gooey people. It's a fucking law of physics that for every action there is an equal and opposite reaction. The pendulum could swing back the other way on all of this. I see it happening already, and it gives me some hope. Commercials are starting to go in divergent directions. For every one of the aforementioned commercials featuring puppies in cars made with love, I see an ad for a UFC pay-per-view. A select few heroes are pushing back against the softening trend and going to extremes—jumping off glaciers, doing Spartan challenges, and getting into the Octagon.

I'm starting to have a lot of conversations with young men about what the fuck is wrong with other young men. I recently had a talk with a young employee who lamented that the rest of his coworkers were such lazy, soft, thin-skinned, entitled shits. I agreed but told him that the good news was that all he had to be was willing to show up, and to work and deal effectively with criticism, and he would be a model employee. The basics of yesteryear would make him an all-star. In the land of the lazy, the competent will be king. Things are starting to turn. It feels like when you're hungover and you've just had your first good puke. You're starting to feel a little relief; you know it's not over yet, but it's the beginning of the end.

If the toughness trend continues but doesn't make the shitty course we're on tap out, I fear that we'll end up evolving into two very different species. There will be one species called *Homo octagonus* and another called *Homo safespacian*. *Homo octagonus* will literally have thick skin, like leather or burlap. They will have evolved from the people who challenged themselves to be better instead of blaming others, who fasted and dove into cold pools, who, when insulted, punched people at a bar instead of calling HR. Their entire body will be covered in calluses. They'll turn on whichever viewing device is invented in their time and hear, "Welcome to the Bukkake Cage Fighting Network. We realize there are many other channels devoted to bukkake and cage fighting, but we were the first."

*Homo safespacians* will live in dwellings made entirely of Nerf and bubble wrap, because millennia of oversensitivity left them literally with thin skin. That supersensitive skin on your belly will cover their entire body. It will be as thin as the seaweed that wraps sushi rolls and will be transparent, showing their organs. Of course, they will have no sex organs. Having an identifiable gender would be an attack. They will have no teeth, because centuries of a Yummy Phase–based diet will have rendered them useless. When they turn on the TV, they'll hear, "Welcome to MSNBCLGBTQ. Tonight: Is your veggie wash racist?" The opposite of dogs who can hear a wider range of frequencies, they will be deaf to everything except that with which they agree. The good news is that, like Neanderthals, this species will eventually die out, because in their never-ending hunting and gathering of insults to confirm their victim status, they'll turn on one another in a slow, civil genocide of microaggressions.

## The Death of Death

I would love to think that this grim look into the future won't matter because I won't be around to see it, but that might not actually be the case, given the rise of celebrity holograms. Shortly after Tupac made his holographic comeback playing Coachella, Amy Winehouse, Roy Orbison, Frank Zappa, Michael Jackson, Billie Holiday, and Whitney Houston all rose from the dead and went on tour. At least their greedy fucking families did. Even "The Gipper," Ronald Reagan, is now back welcoming you to his library in Simi Valley. I would love to go there and shout, "Look out, it's the hologram of John Hinckley!"

The families are trying to make a couple of bucks trampling on the memories of their more talented relatives. Last year the family of James Dean said they would allow his image to be used to create a wholly digital character in a new movie. This is scary. My kids would definitely be like, "Yes, before he died he expressed an interest in doing gay porn. How much did you say you'd pay the estate again?"

Our dark and disgusting future will be one in which we're never going to have to mourn anybody, because everybody will be alive in hologram form. As an atheist who believes life is short and that we should make the best of it while we can, I hate this idea. Life is not supposed to go on forever. It's supposed to be fleeting and, therefore, embraced. That said, after he passes, I will strongly get behind the idea of Holo-Graham Parker.

Since I'm on the topic of death, how about the last words for this book?

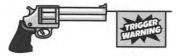

One last trigger warning in this final chapter, because I want to get away from that shit. I hope we stop being triggered in general. Being triggered robs you of your life.

Think about when you're in traffic and someone cuts you off. If you count to ten Mississippi instead of immediately flipping the guy off and honking your horn, that anger will probably subside. You don't need half a day or even a fifteen-minute call with your therapist. One verse of the song you're listening to on the radio is enough time for the microstorm in your soul to pass.

Cue Caine's flute music from *Kung Fu* and dig this metaphor on being triggered. Imagine that a fly lands on your nose. If you can wait five seconds before swatting at it, that fly will be gone. It will just fly away. If you take a whack at it, you'll just end up hitting your nose. So, live your life like you are holding two pies. That way if that same fly lands on your nose, you can't swat at it—because if you do, you won't get the fly; you'll get the pie.

The undercurrent of all my beefs in this book is fear. That's the bottom line of this shitty era we live in. Fear.

You can tell because the culture doth protest too much, methinks. Every era has a buzzword or two. If you go back to the '50s, it was all "rocket," "jet," and "atomic." A kid would buy a baseball mitt and it would be The Rocket Glove. His little red wagon would be "jet-powered." In the '60s, everything was "space age." The tinfoil that people had been using for decades was now a "space-age alloy." The space-age thing hung on a little into the '70s with the moon landing being in '69, but in the later '70s everything slowed down when people were told to "keep on truckin'" and were saying "ten-four" to their good buddies in the convoy during the CB radio craze. In the '80s, we got back up to speed with "turbo." Everything was "turbocharged," and not just your car—your vacuum, your cologne, and your laxative were all "turbocharged." In the '90s, after the Stealth Bomber debuted (or did it?????), everything was either "stealth" or "mach." The razor in your medicine cabinet was "stealth," and so was the vibrator under your bed. That vibrator was gonna give you an orgasm before you knew what was coming, literally. Dodge had a car called the Stealth; it was a piece of shit, but it was "stealth." In the 2000s, with the advent of the X Games, everything was "extreme," or rather, "Xtreme." Everything from Mountain Dew to H&R Block's home accounting software was "extreme!!!!!"

"Brave" is the buzzword for this era. This is obviously pushback against the idea that we know we've gone full-blown puss. The other version of this idea that I see everywhere is "fearless." Recently, I saw a magazine cover featuring Chrissy Teigen with the headline, "Food, Family & Being Fearless." Yeah, talking shit about Trump on Twitter and making scones with brown bananas—*fearless*!!!

You know who was truly fearless and brave? Jimmy Doolittle. (For those of you who think I'm talking about the doctor who could talk to animals first, ( Google It ) **bit.ly/ESA-Doolittle** and then kill yourself.) Our navy had been decimated by the Japs during the attack on Pearl Harbor. He decided we needed to strike back. We weren't geared up for a strategic victory, but we needed a moral victory. We were going to get an aircraft carrier as close to Tokyo as possible, fly B-25 Mitchell medium bombers, and do a run knowing that we didn't have enough fuel to get back. This was a suicide mission, and Doolittle volunteered to lead it. That's fearless.

Anyone who listens to my podcast knows I'm a big fan of the Albert Brooks movie *Defending Your Life*. There are movies that make you laugh, like *Tropic Thunder*. There are movies that make you cry, like *Brian's Song*. And there are movies that make you think, like *Crimes and Misdemeanors*. This is one movie that does all three. (Along with the 1986 Stallone masterpiece *Cobra*. My next book will be a Malcolm Gladwell–esque three-hundred-page breakdown of that movie—nay, film.) I would call *Defending Your Life* an important movie. In short, an advertising executive played by Brooks dies in a car accident and wakes up in an afterlife where he must prove in a courtlike setting that he successfully conquered fear while existing as a human on Earth. If he succeeds, he will go "onward." If not, he will be sent back to Earth to inhabit a new persona and try again. In the movie, the recently deceased earthlings are called "little brains" by the residents of Judgment City, because they use only 3 to 5 percent of their brains and that 3 to 5 percent is consumed by fear. It's funny because it's true. This is what makes Brooks's movie brilliant. The more your life is focused on dealing with fear, the dumber you are. The news media, the politicians, and the true-crime show producers are trying to scare you into giving them your money, and in the case of social media, your attention and personal information. The more susceptible you are to that fear, the dumber you are and the more of your life you're wasting. Albert Brooks's character, Daniel, has an attorney named Bob Diamond, played perfectly by Rip Torn. He tells Daniel the following about life on Earth:

*Fear is like a giant fog. It sits on your brain and blocks everything— real feelings, true happiness, real joy. They can't get through that fog. But you lift it, and buddy, you're in for the ride of your life.*

I'm not telling you to liquidate your house and the kid's college fund to open a business offering zip line tours of the rainforest canopy. That may not work out. And I'm not telling you to take a stroll through bear country chomping on beef jerky wearing your Beats by Dre headphones. You're going to get eaten. Being fearless doesn't mean putting yourself in danger. Evel Knievel was fearless, but he was also in traction half of his life. Being fearless isn't about not feeling fear; it's about mitigating fear. The happiest and calmest guys I've ever met are Indy car and mixed-martial-arts guys. If you are attracted to those activities, you have already learned to master your fear. But the Indy guy wouldn't want to get in an Octagon, and the MMA guy wouldn't want to get behind the wheel of an Indy car. They understand their strengths and weaknesses and what their passions are, and haven't let their fears hold them back from achieving greatness in their chosen fields. That's fearless. That's brave. It's about weighing a risk and embarking on a venture despite that risk—taking that leap of faith that you might not succeed but goddammit you're going to try.

We've been trained to be triggered by the mass media and Madison Avenue, by professors and politicians. We've been trained to live as if we are victims, that our power resides outside ourselves in the form of our support animals or in the group that we've identified ourselves as part of, even if that group is just a bunch of people using the same hashtag. This book isn't about how the shitshow our society has become is inconveniencing me. It's about—ironically, given the last few paragraphs—my fear that we won't be able to turn this ship around and that we won't have a society left for me to complain about.

I've talked a ton of shit about a lot of people and about society in this book. If you were triggered by it, if you felt like I was victim blaming, if you felt like you deserve an apology, if you felt like creating an anti-Adam hashtag or going to a safe space with your emotional support animal, then clearly you weren't reading closely enough. I wasn't yelling *at* you; I was yelling *for* you.

# *Epilogue*

## Coronavirus Panic and Pandemic

This book was done. It was edited, proofread, and designed. I was recording the audiobook. Two days before it went to the printer, the COVID-19 virus brought the United States to a complete standstill.

Whenever this book gets into your hands—which will have been washed 278,000 times, meaning you have sung "Happy Birthday" 556,000 times or the equivalent of three Phish songs—who knows what the fuck will be going on? All of our social distancing and business-shuttering may have kept the virus at bay and we'll have flattened the curve (and as a man who likes the busty chicks, I hate the idea of flattening any curves). Or it could be worse than predicted and we could be living in underground caverns like *The Mole People*, a movie written by my step-grandfather László Görög. ( Google It ) **https://bit.ly/ESA-Mole** So, at the time of this writing, these are my thoughts. They may prove to be prescient or insane. But no matter what happens when the infected dust settles, this virus will have brought out the worst—and hopefully some of the best—of the fucked-up culture I just spent 200 pages trashing.

There was opportunity in this crisis. It happened, we were powerless, and we had to make the most of it. In prison, there's a saying: "You can do the time or the time can do you." (I learned that when I was doing seventeen months for soliciting a min... never mind.) This lockdown is like a short prison sentence. If you let the time do you, you're going to end up with a face tattoo and a toilet full of Pruno. Or, if you do the time, you could read, or perhaps write, the great American novel. (Sorry, I've already written the great American nonfiction book, which you're in the midst of thumbing through right now.) This was a time to go out and build a treehouse with your son, or to cook lasagna with your wife and daughter. I interviewed the great Kevin Bacon during the midst of the shutdown and he said he did a puzzle with his wife for the first time ever. Again, you're doing the time no matter what. You could come out with a great novel or a venereal disease.

During the first weekend of "shelter in place," I was hiking with my son, seeing all the people getting some fresh air, and realized that this was a sort of forced sabbath for atheists. When you have a religion, there are specific days, sometimes weeks, and sometimes even full months where you have to not use electricity, not eat meat, go to your house of worship, and spend time with family. The thing you're not doing is hauling your ass to Cleveland to do stand-up. For an atheist like myself, every day is potentially a work day. But this forced everything to slow down. And it felt good. If there's a positive yin to the pandemic yang, this is it. Not only that, but for a few sweet blissful days, while everyone was hunkering down, L.A. became an *Omega Man* style ghost town where there was no traffic. This was utopia for me as I headed to my last set at the Laugh Factory before everyone closed up shop.

To my earlier point about fear, the real pandemic is people, mostly white people, panicking. That spread further, wider, and much faster than the virus ever did. This was hysteria in the truest sense of the word. I talked many times in this book about how we fell into "chick-think." I was delighted when Dr. Drew informed me that hysteria comes from the same root word as hysterectomy. *Hyster* is Greek for the uterus. We all literally became chicks.

Coronavirus is to the flu as school shootings are to shootings in the inner city. We're familiar with the flu. We have the knowledge that it's not likely to kill you unless you're old or infirm, and we've been hearing about it for a while. Same with inner city shootings. We've been hearing about them since the '70s and got immune to it when, by pure numbers, many more die of gang-related violence in Chicago in one week than die in school shootings in a year. This pandemic exposed a major flaw in our society that I've long complained about. We, literally, can't do the math. All of our problems, many of which I laid out in this book, are fueled by feelings rather than facts. We have data that we are ignoring.

The news is complicit in this. It's their job to scare the crap out of you. In this case, they literally scared the crap out of people enough that there was a run on toilet paper. People were getting into fist fights over Charmin. The paper goods section turned into *The Jerry Springer Show*. What happened to dignity? You're choking a bitch over some two-ply. You're supposed to be dueling with pistols at dawn when someone offends your honor, not duking it out in aisle eleven at the Stop and Shop. We have laws against gouging. If a hurricane comes through, I'm not allowed to go to Home Depot, load up on one hundred sheets of plywood at $34 a sheet and charge you $150. But we have no rules around hoarding. Dr. Drew's wife, the whitest, least meth-y looking woman on the planet, tried to buy two boxes of Sudafed and was stopped in her tracks. As if the middle-aged lady from Pasadena was making trucker speed in her bathtub. There are rules. There should be some for hoarding. If you try to walk out of the Kroger with twenty-eight packs of Angel Soft, someone should stop you and say, "How many assholes do you have? Are you Mormon? Is this for all the sister wives?" I understand if it were D-cell batteries, ammunition, and cans of beans, but why toilet paper as your apocalypse hoarding item? (I guess if you ate all those beans you'd need it.) I feel like I could go a year without using toilet paper if I needed to. It would be rough, but I could do it. I'd start with the spent tube socks and eventually work my way to my dog's tail.

To that end, if by the time you read this we are still the freaked-out, narcissistic dicks and cunts we were at the beginning of this panic, and if there's still empty toilet paper shelves at the grocery store, please cut out and enjoy the following page of custom Carolla TP...assuming you weren't an asswipe who hoarded all the asswipe.

# Acknowledgments

I must thank Anthony Ziccardi and Post Hill for being *brave* and *fearless* enough to take on a book my old publishers and others in New York were too woke to touch. I'd like to thank my editor Jacob Hoye for his hard work and collaboration. I'd also like to shout out my assistant Matt Fondiler—who I usually shout at— for sending and reading a thousand emails related to this project. And finally, a tip of the cap to archivist Superfan Giovanni for his assistance with…well, he knows what he did.

# About the Author

Adam Carolla is the author of the *New York Times* bestsellers *In Fifty Years We'll All Be Chicks, Not Taco Bell Material, President Me,* and *Daddy, Stop Talking!,* as well as a radio and television host, a comedian, and an actor. Carolla is well known as the cohost of the syndicated radio and MTV show *Loveline,* the cocreator and star of *The Man Show* and *Crank Yankers,* and a contestant on *Dancing with the Stars* and *The Celebrity Apprentice.* He currently hosts *The Adam Carolla Show,* which is the Guinness World Record holder for Most Downloaded Podcast and is available on iTunes and AdamCarolla.com.